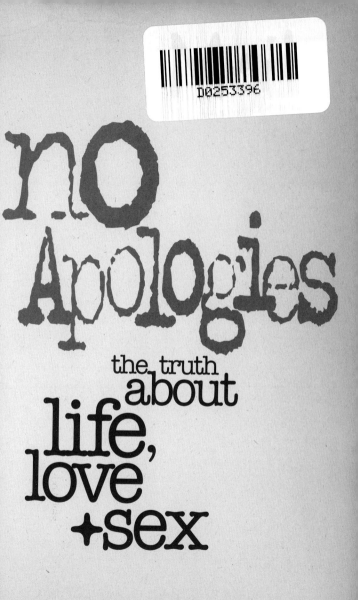

no
Apologies

the truth
about
life,
love
+sex

lisM

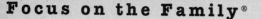
Focus on the Family®

LiFE on the EdGe™

no Apologies

the truth about life, love +sex

TYNDALE

Tyndale House Publishers, Wheaton, Illinois

NO APOLOGIES: THE TRUTH ABOUT LIFE, LOVE AND SEX
Copyright © 1999 by Focus on the Family
All rights reserved. International copyright secured.

Library of Congress Cataloging-in-Publication Data
No apologies : a message from Focus on the Family.
        p.   cm.
    "A Focus on the Family book"—T.p. verso.
    Includes bibliographical references.
    Summary: Provides the facts about sex, highlighting
abstinence as the only true "safe sex." with testimony from
real people about how choices of pre-marital sex have
affected their lives.
    ISBN 1-56179-654-9
        1. Teenagers—United States—Sexual behavior Juvenile
literature.   2. Premarital sex—United States Juvenile literature.
3. Sexual abstinence—United States Juvenile literature.
[1. Youth—Sexual behavior.   2. Sexual abstinence.   3. Sexual
ethics.]   I. Focus on the Family (Organization)
HQ27.N6   1999
306.7'083—dc21—dc21   99-12969
[306.7'083]   CIP

A Focus on the Family book published by
Tyndale House Publishers, Wheaton, Illinois

Cover Design: Mark Boswell
Printed in the United States of America
99 00 01 02 03/10 9 8 7 6 5 4 3 2

Contents

1

Serious Business

Things always look different in the morning. But in all her life Jennifer had never imagined it would look like *this*.

You love me, don't you? If you love me, you'll let me.

What are you worrying about?—I've got a condom.

All the snappy comebacks she could have thrown at Jason's lines ran through her head—like, *If YOU loved ME you'd show me some respect.* For whatever reason, they hadn't occurred to her at the time.

Why had she let it happen? Somehow it all seemed so different at the time: the warmth, the closeness, the exciting secrecy and forbiddenness of it all. The romance and exhilaration of two young lovers against the world. And now…the cold light of day. And everything so very, very different. How could everything change so quickly?

Jen stopped mid-thought and found herself staring, through a blur of tears, at the big brown teddy bear sitting on the shelf against the opposite wall. She threw back the covers, jumped out of bed, locked herself in the bathroom, and took a long, hot shower.

◎　◎　◎

Pound, pound, pound. Incessant feet against unyielding pavement. Jason found that jogging was one way to shut out thoughts and feelings. *Back to normal,* he thought. (Breathe, stride, step.) *Back into the groove. Everything normal. Everything the way it was.* With every stride he wished it as hard as he could.

Beautiful Jenny. He had believed it when he told her that he loved her. He had! The pounding of his feet did nothing to banish the vision: Even now he could feel the smoothness of her skin, smell the fragrance of her hair. In her presence it was as if something took control of his mind and body.

He wanted her.

He got what he wanted.

And now? He didn't know, but he thought he wanted out.

It *was* possible, wasn't it? To be free, to feel like a kid again? Nobody—none of the other guys who bragged about "scoring"— had warned him about this. They acted as if sex was something you picked up and put down, like a can of beer at last night's party. No one had told him about the hook, the chain, the feeling of being in over your head.

Jason passed the pale green stucco house a second time and thought about his mom making breakfast in the kitchen. *As if everything is the same. But it isn't.* The rusted swing set where he and his sister used to play jutted just above the backyard fence. Rounding the corner under the bare elms, he started his third lap around the block. *Too much to think about.* He'd throw himself into track and studies and steer clear from Jenny for a while.

◎ ◎ ◎

Jen pushed a strand of dark hair back from her face and scraped her chair closer to the library table. Hushed whispers all around; musty smell of old books. She stared at the text in front of her: *"Beowulf"? ... what's up with that? I thought this was an ENGLISH Lit class ...* She was tired of feeling dumb, ugly, and nauseated.

Jason had been making himself scarce. It was strange, in a way, after all the months of intense togetherness. But then she wasn't really surprised. *With him,* she thought, *it was all a game. All lies. What did I expect? I'll never trust a guy again.* She hated him—but at the same time missed the comfortable feeling of his nearness.

Where else would she go to find that feeling?

"Jen," came a voice at her ear. "I'm sorry. Did I startle you? Can we talk?"

She turned to see Jason crouching beside her chair, his dark eyes serious. "Oh, it's *you*." Her whisper sounded harsh. "I hardly recognized you, it's been so long."

"Jen, I'm not what you think I am. Really. You've got me all wrong."

"You've got *me* wrong if you think I'll be fooled again."

"Let me explain. I've been doing a lot of thinking. I know I was unfair to you, and—"

"Think again, Jason. And let *me* explain something." She glanced around the room, then went on in a lower tone. "I got hold of one of those at-home pregnancy tests."

"You *what?*"

"Mm-hm," she said. "And guess what? It was positive."

He looked blank. "But—is it right? I mean, can you trust it?"

"*I* do," she answered. "At least as much as you trust condoms."

◎　◎　◎

No Middle Ground

Sex is going to come up in everybody's life. It's a matter of

4

*life. And nowadays, it's also a
matter of death.*
—Jack (18)

*I believe that sexuality is the
number one topic that kids are
really struggling with across the
board.*
—Mike Ashburn, Young Life

Sex. It seems as though everybody's thinking about it, everybody's talking about it. A person's sexuality is a crucial part of growing up—a critical, strategic piece in the complex puzzle of every individual's life. If it hasn't impacted you yet, you can bet your time is coming. It's not a question of *if*, but of *when* and *how*.

And note this: The way you answer the *when* and *how* questions will make all the difference. Depending on your answers to those questions, sex can be either a central part of the most beautiful, fulfilling, and deeply meaningful of all human relationships, or a source of lifelong frustration, anguish, and pain.

It might even kill you.

No Apologies: The Truth About Life, Love, and Sex is a book for teens—and singles of *all* ages—who want to think seriously about the *what*, *when*, and *how* of their own sexuality. It's an attempt to communicate the vital message that there's only one correct solution to the puzzle. Put the pieces together correctly, each in its proper place, and they make a beautiful picture. Separate them, isolate them, mix and match them, or throw them together at random, and you get chaos and fragmentation. Because sex outside the context for which it was designed—sex without love, without permanence, without commitment, without regard for the delicate balance and fragile web of life—can be dangerous and destructive.

You heard right. There really *is* only one correct answer to the question, "How should I handle the sexual side of my life?" Such a statement can't help but rub a lot of people the wrong way in this era of tolerance, plurality, and relative truth. But it's a statement that desperately needs to be made. Believe it or not, sex is a lot more like algebra or chemistry than poetry or interpretive dance. You either get it right or you get it wrong. If you get it wrong, there could be an explosion. When it comes to your choice of a sexual partner, there isn't a whole lot of room for personal preference or style; no question of "what's right for me" being something different from "what's right for you."

It's the purpose of this book to hold up that one correct answer for every reader to see—to state it clearly, argue it, examine it, expand it, and, most importantly, *celebrate* it. Because sex, when you get it *right*, really is something worth getting excited about.

Sex is serious business. It's like nuclear energy. Correctly channeled and controlled, it's one of the closest things to a miracle we'll ever encounter in normal human life. Handled carelessly, it can cause unspeakable damage and devastation. There is no middle ground.

The Personal Side
If you don't believe that, just listen to the people who have been there and found it out for themselves: the Jasons and Jennifers who know from experience that sex is not simply a casual, "recreational" activity. They know now. It's abundantly clear. But there's no going back.

Jason and Jennifer are not merely fictional characters. They're your friends. Your classmates. Your brothers and sisters. The kids next door and down the street. The kids who sit next to you in Biology or hang out with your church youth group.

They might even be you.

Whoever they are, they've discovered

7

that sex is a force that changes a person's life in dramatic and permanent ways. You'll meet some of them in the chapters to come. Their stories show a side of premarital sexual activity that isn't often represented in Sex Ed texts or steamy network dramas.

Stories like Adrienne's, for instance. Adrienne believed her friends when they told her "everybody's doing it." The ironic thing is that she actually cared less about her boyfriend and the physical pleasures of sex than she did about being "cool" and satisfying her curiosity. She didn't take sex seriously. She dabbled in it and played around with it. And she ended up paying a huge price. Adrienne's life today is vastly different from anything she could have pictured just a few years ago.

And Sarah. Sarah got carried away with her feelings. She let feelings persuade her to toss out big chunks of everything she had ever believed about sex, self-esteem, and the right way to live, just because she met a certain guy. The real twist came when she discovered—the *hard* way—that he wasn't the guy of her dreams after all. She gave up everything for him only to see it all trampled underfoot. And in the end Sarah was left on her own, hurt and struggling, facing an uncertain future. That experience and its practical aftermath have changed everything for Sarah. And all because sex, as she now knows only too well, is something more—something *much* more—than just "a feeling about a feeling."

Then there's Leslie. Leslie's problem was naïveté. At 16 years of age, she hadn't given sexuality or the possibility of premarital sexual activity much thought. On the surface, the subject didn't concern her—she had lots of other things on her mind. But Leslie's innocence, combined with another weak spot in her character, eventually led her off the road and into a ditch. The desperate desire to feel loved started her down the wrong road. If only she'd known that you can't get love by giving sex.

It *never* works that way. She knows it now.

Or Jack. Jack's the kind of guy who seems to know better; the kind of guy who says one thing and does another thing—and doesn't see it as a problem. He'll tell you that virginity is a precious gift to be carefully preserved and guarded; that premarital sex can be "devastating"; that abstinence is the best way to protect yourself against pregnancy and disease and emotional trauma. The strange thing is that none of this has stopped *him* being sexually active. He's probably not alone.

The Goal: Devising a Plan

Adrienne, Sarah, Leslie, and Jack—and a number of others who can tell us something about the power of sex—will all have a chance to speak for themselves at greater length in the pages that follow. As their stories unfold, watch for the thread that links them. Each one of them, in its own way, points to a simple truth. Sex cuts to the heart of life itself. It is an unbelievably powerful, life-altering, mind-bending force. God created it that way. For that reason, sex *must* be handled according to a careful plan of action. When it is, the result is wholeness, satisfaction, and real joy. When it isn't, disaster follows.

By the time you get to the last page of this book you will have heard this message presented in perhaps a hundred different ways. Don't miss the point. Everybody needs to think about how he or she will deal with the powerful mystery of sex *before* crucial decisions must be made. Everyone should have a plan of action in place and understand why it's been adopted *before* the storm of sexual urges and feelings breaks over his head.

Thoughtless passion usually comes with a hefty price tag. Surprise pregnancy. Forfeited educational and career goals. Loss of personal freedom. A lifelong sense of betrayal. Guilt about using and abusing someone else. Anger. Remorse. The tragedy of abortion. Broken relationships, shattered hopes and dreams, faded love. Disease, discomfort, even death. And the enduring pain of the impotent apologies—the feeling that no matter how hard you try, you can never make things right again.

Some or all of the above can be yours if you wade into the current of sexual activity without *thinking* about what you're doing. I'm reminded of the family that put a rubber raft into Central Oregon's unpredictable Deschutes River a couple of years ago. They picked a glassy stretch of water for their launch on a bright Saturday. Just the right amount of current for a nice ride. But they had no idea at all what awaited them just a half mile downstream. They hadn't heard about Dillon Falls. They never imagined themselves perishing under the raging waters. They never imagined their little boy clinging to a rock for three hours until rescuers arrived. The fact is, they'd never even thought to look at a map. And when they saw the signs along the river that warned them to turn back, they just ignored them.

It's much the same with your sexual future. If you take the time to check out the landmarks and terrain, and plot out a wise itinerary, your journey through the regions of life, love, romance, and sex can be intensely enjoyable and fulfilling. But you have to know something about the river before you launch. It isn't optional. It's life or death. Any guide will tell you that.

Don't learn that lesson the hard way. Don't follow Jason and Jennifer into the wilderness of regret and confusion. How much better to have in place a plan for avoiding the fear, uncertainty, and unyielding pain! How much better to put ourselves in a place where we don't need to apologize!

◎ ◎ ◎

Evening at the Espresso Bar. Together again over cappuccino, Jason and Jennifer wage an intimate and painful war of looks and words. Glasses clink, the air pungent with the smell of coffee, the room humming with conversation. Her resentment steams like the espresso machine. He struggles under a burden of guilt and responsibility, love and desperation, a helpless desire to fix what's broken. He thinks he has a plan. She wavers between hatred and insecurity.

"Why are you stressing?" he says. "What's the big deal? We'll just get married…. I'll go to work during the day and finish school at night. You can stay home with the baby...."

"Oh, yeah!" she answers. "And condoms always work. So now marriage will solve everything! Is that what you think? You don't get to decide that. What about *me*? What am I supposed to say to my parents? 'Mom, Dad, I won't be going to college because I'm pregnant, but it's okay—Jason and I are getting married!' I don't think so!"

He shifts uncomfortably, his face a picture of exasperation. Drawing in a quick breath, he tries another tack.

"Look, Jen, I don't want this baby to grow up without a dad. I know what that feels like—believe me."

"Oh, spare me. Has anyone ever told you that babies cost money? I don't have any. Do *you*?"

"No, but...there's welfare and stuff ... and we'll get by—"

"Oh, perfect! Welfare! That's a great way to raise a kid! You're just full of great ideas, Jason."

"Jen, I don't know what you want me to say here...."

"I think you've said plenty...more than enough. But *this* time I am going to have a say in what happens."

He looks beaten and confused and

searches the room for some sign, some symbol of stability or confidence. He decides to back off and try to smooth the waters.

"Okay," he says quietly. "I'm sorry. Just relax—all right?"

"Sorry's not enough, Jason," she replies. "It's too late to apologize."

2

Influences

Steve sat fidgeting and glancing at his watch. It was already past seven, and the basketball game was scheduled to start at seven-thirty—across town. Had she completely forgotten?

The door to the coffee shop suddenly banged open and the bell announced the arrival of three more customers. Steve looked up at the sound of loud laughter and saw Sarah enter the shop with Kevin and Cindy—all three of them silly, giddy, giggling, and unsteady on their feet. He groaned and turned back to his table.

"Hey, Stevie!" she said, approaching from behind and covering his eyes with her hands. "Ready for some fun?"

He pulled away and faced her. "What's up with you, Sarah?" he demanded. "You were supposed to be here over an hour ago. What are you doing with Kevin, anyway?"

"Well...," she drawled, rolling her eyes in the direction of her two friends with a stupid smile, "Kevin and Cindy got hold of a bottle of vodka...and so we came to find you...."

"You came to find *me*?" he asked, eyeing her two companions with distaste. "So what do you want to do now?"

"Whatever *you* want to do," she replied, batting her lashes and running the fingers of one hand through his hair. "You know, my parents aren't home tonight...and there's still some vodka left...."

◎　◎　◎

Have you noticed? Empty spaces don't stay that way for long. Let the grass die and the dandelions take over. Get rid of the cat and the mice move in. Neglect a leak and the ship sinks. Leave a hole or a gap somewhere and *something* will come along to fill it.

That's especially true of empty heads.

A thoughtless and clueless mind is a dangerous thing. It doesn't stay empty for long. It tends to get filled up with whatever happens to be roaming the streets in the neighborhood. In the absence of a strategy, conviction, or conscious commitment to a carefully chosen course of action, it's anybody's guess which of the hundreds of outside influences competing for control of our mental and physical energies will come out on top. And there's no telling what might happen once a winner emerges.

Jesus illustrated this principle in Matthew 12:43-45. It's good to cast an evil spirit out of a demon-possessed man, He said. But if something (or Someone) better doesn't immediately move in to take that demon's place, it's likely to return—this time with a few nasty friends. It's the same with bad habits and false ideas. Obviously, the bad *has* to go. But ridding ourselves of negative things is only half the job. It's not enough to leave the house of our mind swept clean and empty. It needs to be occupied and filled with something positive and active. Otherwise, we'll find ourselves faced with a long line of unsavory applicants for the vacancy.

What about you? When it comes to sex, are you under the control of healthful, wholesome, rational, and sensible attitudes and values? Or has. someone or something else—something foreign, unfriendly, and less than conducive to your well-being—taken charge of the situation? Any landlord will tell you it's much easier to move tenants in than to move them *out*. It's important to take stock of the outside influences that can come in and take charge of an empty room with nobody upstairs at the controls. Let's look at a few of them.

Peer Pressure

> *I believe it's extremely hard to*
> *abstain. In my old high school,*
> *most of the kids have sex by the*
> *time they're seniors.*
> —Mark (15)

If you don't want to think for yourself, it's usually pretty easy to find other people eager to do it for you. To a certain extent, the approval of friends and peers powerfully influences all of us, but their influence is especially strong when we're young. Besides, there's no great investment of thought or energy required of those who follow the group. It takes no effort at all to go with the flow.

Friends and peers had a lot to do with the loss of Adrienne's virginity. In fact, friends exerted a much bigger impact on her life than she ever thought possible. She and her boyfriend hadn't talked directly about sex.

Neither of them had been sexually active. After five months of going together, they still hadn't discussed the subject of boundaries or limits: what they wanted to do, just how far they would or wouldn't go. But they *had* been moving with a group of people who seemed to take sex for granted—people who talked openly every day about sexual encounters and adventures. This casual attitude toward sex made all the difference to Adrienne and her boyfriend. The easiest thing in the world to do is drift with the crowd.

"I remember my best friend in high school," Adrienne said. "We all used to go together to visit her boyfriend at his apartment. When the two of them decided it was time to have sex, they'd kick all of us out onto the porch. We'd have to sit outside until they were done, and then they'd let us come back in and be with them again."

With friends like that, it was only natural that Adrienne and her boyfriend eventually found themselves in bed together. When it happened, her girlfriends threw a party for her to celebrate and commemorate a life-changing event that just *had* to happen—a rite of passage in the life of a young girl. Adrienne had lost her virginity and her friends were proud of her. The peer group was pleased.

"I do think teenagers are pushed into having sex because of peer pressure," she says. "But it's more than that. With me, it was that all my friends were having sex and I thought it was okay. I didn't necessarily see anything wrong with it. It wasn't something that bothered any of my friends. There was just an atmosphere of acceptance about it."

Joanna Thompson, National Coordinator of Care for the Family in the United Kingdom, understands. She says, "I would really like teenagers to ask themselves this question—'Why do I *want* to be sexually active?'—and to ask that question honestly, because, for many of them, the answer would be one of two things: either they are trying to keep their partner or they are simply doing what the rest of their peer group is doing. Very few of them do this because it's what they really *want* to do."

Maybe that's why Adrienne, unlike some other girls, didn't feel dirty and used and remorseful the morning after. Her immediate experience was something very different. "At the time, I thought it was pretty cool. I didn't wake up the next day and regret doing it. I continued doing it for a long time before it started to bother me that I was having sex." But whether she knew it or not, Adrienne's life was now moving in a new direction.

She'd merged from one highway into another, heading for a destination she'd never considered—a direction she never would have consciously chosen.

"I talk to teens today," says Adrienne, "because there are a lot of things I wish I had heard in high school that nobody ever took the time to say to me. I wish somebody would have told me that it's okay *not* to have sex."

Counselor and youth worker Michelle Baranek invests a lot of time and energy in doing just that. Michelle's perspective on the subject of teens, sex, and peer pressure is this: "What influences teen behavior today is peers...or what you perceive your peers are doing. *Not* every teen is doing it. The majority of our teens in high school are virgins."

Assumptions, Presumptions, and Expectations

> *They tell you that you can have sex. I don't think they really care about kids—I mean, that just shows they don't care. And maybe the companies want to make money or something like that. I think it's a sign that they don't care.*
>
> —Rob (17)

Whether we're good at handling it or not, most of us are aware of the power of peer pressure. Everybody assumes that friends and their opinions about what's cool and uncool are pretty important. But what about parents, teachers, authority figures, and other adults? Do *their* attitudes and expectations have any influence over the lives of teenagers?

Obviously they do. And very often that influence is helpful and positive. But any teen who wants to be smart about sex needs to realize that situations can arise in which the expectations and assumptions of adults may be just as destructive and misleading as pressure from peers. It all depends on who those adults are, what they think about sex outside of marriage, and how they communicate their views.

Think of it this way. Every good educator knows the power of teacher expectations, whether for good or ill. Convince Johnny that he has an unusually good head for numbers and his math scores will probably begin to soar. Cover his papers with red ink, reassign him to a seat in "the vegetable row," and he'll get used to the idea that he's a failure. Whether we know it or not, we're all looking for someone to tell us who we are and what we can—and should—do. We are sensitive to praise and criticism. Even hints or suggestions from people we perceive as powerful, authoritative, or worthy of our respect can have a huge impact on our attitude and outlook.

In the same way, the messages adults communicate about sex exert a subtle but strong effect upon the incidence of sexual activity among teens. It happens in a couple of different ways.

Adults Who Say Too Little

Adults may know what's right and fully understand what their kids need to hear…but they're uncomfortable with the subject and afraid to talk about it. So they clam up. Or make an impersonal appeal to tradition and taboo: "Just don't do it. It's wrong. In my day, only sluts got pregnant in their teens."

Adrienne has an interesting perspective on adults who adopt this approach. "Teens become sexually active for a number of reasons," she observes. "One is curiosity. A lot of teens just wonder what all the hype is about. They think, *What is this sex thing that makes so many adults just squirm in their chairs? There has to be something exciting or fun there if it can get adults all excited like that.*"

Jack agrees. "In my opinion, teens want to be sexually active because it's forbidden.

There are so many rules and things. I find that a lot of adults are saying, 'Don't have sex'—you know, whether it be religious or a personal opinion. Since a lot of people say, 'Don't do it—you can't have that,' it just makes you wonder, *Why can't I? What will happen to me?"*

Adult silence can stimulate unhealthy teen curiosity. And adult rules and regulations—especially *unexplained* rules and regulations—can inspire knee-jerk rebellion. In these ways, well-meaning adults can actually push teens in the direction of sexual experimentation without intending to do so.

Adults Who Say Too Much

But there's another side to the coin of adult influence, and, unfortunately, it's becoming the more common of the two. In fact, it's more than just common—it's established, institutionalized, and, in some cases, even endorsed by the government. It's the philosophy that says, "These kids just can't keep their clothes on. They're going to do it anyway, so we'd better make sure they do it safely." The result? Sex education courses that present extramarital sex in a "non-judgmental" light and school-based health clinics where condoms and other forms of birth-control are distributed to teenagers free of charge.

Former United States Surgeon General

Joycelyn Elders became a powerful and out-spoken proponent of that approach. She left little room for doubt about *her* expectations of teens when she said, "I tell every girl to put a condom in her purse when she goes out on a date."[1] On another occasion she said, "We taught teens what to do in the front seat of a car. Now it's time to teach them what to do in the back seat."[2]

And how did other influential adults feel about Dr. Elders's outspoken views? The president nominated her to the post of sur-geon general and the Congress eventually confirmed her nomination. That's a pretty powerful endorsement. And when Congress finalized the appointment, Senator Paul Wellstone of Minnesota made this comment: "We're talking about a woman who will be a healing force for our country. She'll be the kind of Surgeon General who will unite us and bring us together." Apparently Senator Wellstone had convictions of his own about the inability of teenagers to control their sex-ual passions!

The Sexuality Information and Education Council of the United States (SIECUS) has been another strong advocate of "value-free" sex education in the schools. Early in the 1990s, SIECUS drew up 13 sex education goals to be accomplished by the year 2000 and a set of "Guidelines for Comprehensive Sexuality Education" for grades K-12. In the booklet "Sex Education 2000," SIECUS Executive Director Debra Haffner wrote that "every person has a right to receive sexual information and to consider accepting sexual relationships for pleasure as well as for procreation."

In an article titled "Safe Sex and Teens," Ms. Haffner offered her own unique ideas on the subject of "abstinence":

> We need to tell teens that the safest sex doesn't necessarily mean no sex, but rather behaviors that have no possibility of causing pregnancy or a sexually transmitted disease. A partial list of safe sex practices for teens could include: Talking, Flirting, Dancing, Hugging, Kissing, Necking, Massaging, Caressing, Undressing each other, Masturbation alone, Masturbation in front of a partner, Mutual masturbation. Teens could surely come up with their own list of activities. (p. 9)

Yes, they probably could. Especially with that kind of encouragement!

It's hard to deny that Ms. Haffner's idea

of "abstinence" and the principles of the "safe sex" campaign communicate a powerful unspoken message: Teenagers simply can't control their sexual impulses. That's why senators, surgeons general, government committee members, teachers, and school administrators think they must work so hard to make sure teens are protected—from unwanted pregnancy, from disease...and from themselves. Beat that drum often enough and the message becomes a self-fulfilling prophecy.

Naturally, the promoters of "safe sex" have been telling us from the beginning that free condoms would put a stop to the rising numbers of teen pregnancies. We know now how wrong they were. The incidence of teen pregnancy began to increase almost as soon as they launched their campaign. In an article titled "Condom Roulette," the Family Research Council revealed that unwed pregnancies among 15- to 19-year-olds rose 87 percent between 1970—when Planned Parenthood-type condom distribution programs first began—and 1992. During roughly the same period, teen abortions went up 67 percent[3] and unwed births rose 83.8 percent.[4] One "progressive" high school in Colorado began handing out condoms in 1989, and within three years—by 1992—that school's birthrate had soared to 31 percent above the national average. At that time, 100 births were expected out of only 1,200 students![5]

Meanwhile, thanks in large part to "condomania," we're also facing an unprecedented epidemic of sexually transmitted diseases. A recent study estimates that one in five Americans 12 years of age and over is infected with genital herpes.[6] In addition, infection rates for chlamydia are particularly high among adolescents. In some studies, up to 29 percent of sexually active females ages 12-19 were found to be infected with this organism.[7] Also, there are more than 5.5 million new cases of HPV (human papillomavirus) in the United States each year.[8] These numbers, of course, don't even address the dramatic rise of AIDS and HIV.

So what's the point?

Incredible as it sounds, some teenagers may be allowing themselves to become sexually active because, somewhere deep down inside, *they believe that adults expect it of them.*

Julie (17) doesn't see why teens should mindlessly conform to such expectations. She finds the whole thing insulting. "I think it's a little hypocritical for adults to say that we can't keep our clothes on and that teens are having sex all the time."

She's right. Adults make mistakes too,

and in this case their assumptions are wide of the mark. As Joanna Thompson suggests, teens need to do their own thinking about sex. The subject is too important to be left to anybody else—even well-meaning but misguided adults.

Media

> *I think it is kind of difficult to stay a virgin as a teenager because there is a lot of pressure out there to do those types of things. You know, in movies, magazines. I mean, all the stars. Everybody's doing it.*
>
> —Matt (15)

> *I would say that I think about sex more often than not. I mean, it's a topic everywhere. Look at the schools, look in society. It's on TV. It's everywhere. So it's kind of impossible not to think about it.*
>
> —Jack (18)

Matt's and Jack's comments have never been truer than they are today. And the situation is only intensifying. The entertainment media—movies, pop music, television, magazines, advertising—are jam-packed with sex. Everywhere you turn you find the screen jumping and the airwaves sizzling with sexual references, sexual jokes, sexual innuendoes, even the most graphic portrayals of sexual activity. If your outlook on the world is at all shaped by the media—and it probably is—it's easy to draw Matt's conclusion: "Everybody's doing it."

Just how influential are the media? Consider the following:

- Before kindergarten, the average child views 5,000 hours of TV.
- Half of U.S. children ages 6 to 17 have a TV in their rooms.
- The average child watches 20,000 commercials each year.
- Teens are exposed to 14,000 sexual references and innuendoes on TV annually.

Exactly what kind of input are kids getting during those thousands of hours of television viewing? The answer to that question may explain a lot about their attitudes toward sex.

In early 1998, Warner Brothers' new teen-targeted drama, *Dawson's Creek*, the hippest prime-time hangout on the tube, took only two weeks to set an all-time record for total viewers, ranking just behind NBC's *Seinfeld* as the second-highest rated show among adolescents.

Those statistics take on disturbing significance when you take a close look at the show's content. A single, overriding theme dominates storylines and dialogue: sex. Intercourse, masturbation, genitalia, breasts —all are frequent subjects of conversation among the inhabitants of *Dawson's Creek*. And they're not just talking, either. While Dawson and his childhood friend Joey (short for Josephine) continue to sleep in the bed they've shared since they were seven years old (why stop now just because we have more "body hair"?), his best pal Pacey is involved in a torrid sexual affair with one of his teachers. Meanwhile, Dawson's newest flame, Jen, is revealing the details of her long sexual career, and his mom is engaged in an extracurricular fling with a co-worker.

Just another day in the lives of typical teens, right? Or so the producers would like us to believe.

Dawson's Creek may be the worst of the worst. But anyone who is even slightly familiar with the current TV landscape knows that Dawson doesn't stand alone. The popular sitcom *Frasier* is another place where free and easy sex is taken for granted—as demonstrated in the following scene, where we find Frasier and a lady friend dallying over their dinners in a restaurant:

Frasier: *So how's your appetizer?*

Woman: *Oh, delicious. Your salad?*

Frasier: *It's very good. Ha ha, it's—actually I haven't even tasted it yet.*

Woman: *I hope this doesn't offend you, but I've had the most stressful day, and I really don't have the energy to make a lot of small talk, plus I'm not very hungry. Would you mind terribly....*

Frasier: *So be it. I think I know where this is headed. You don't have to say it.*

Woman: *Frasier, could we just go someplace and have sex?*

Frasier: *Well, that you did have to say.*

Woman: *I'm sorry it sounded forward, but it's the only thing I really want to do right now.*

Frasier: *I'm flattered, and the thought is very tempting, but you see, on my show I'm constantly preaching that people should get to know one another and have things in common before taking that kind of step. What's your favorite color?*

Woman: *Blue.*
Frasier: *Mine too. Check please!*

Then there's music. A study conducted by the American Medical Association indicates that the rock music industry wields almost unbelievably vast power in the lives of most adolescents. "The average teenager," reports the AMA, "listens to 10,500 hours of rock music during the years between the 7th and 12th grades"—that's as many hours as they spend in school from kindergarten through the 12th grade—"and music *surpasses television* as an influence in teenagers' lives."[9] As Gothic death-metal rocker Marilyn Manson put it, "Music is such a powerful medium now. The kids don't even know who the president is, but they know what's on MTV. I think if anyone like Hitler or Mussolini were alive now, they would have to be rock stars."[10]

Sex and eroticism have become standard elements not only of rap, grunge, punk, and heavy metal music, but even of pop, folk, and alternative styles. So explicit are the references to sexual activity in some contemporary lyrics that they can be described only as pornographic. But it hasn't happened overnight. To trace the history of pop music lyrics over the past 30 to 40 years is to rehearse a tale of gradual but steady moral disintegration within popular culture. The titles of some of the biggest hits of the past few decades say it all:

- 1964—The Beatles sing "I Want to Hold Your Hand."
- 1967—The Rolling Stones make a much bolder overture with "Let's Spend the Night Together."
- 1972—The Raspberries encourage the object of their affection to "Go All the Way."
- 1975—Metaphorically speaking, Jethro Tull looks forward to a "Bungle in the Jungle."
- 1981—Even more to the point, Olivia Newton-John beckons a lover to get "Physical."
- 1987—Inhibitions and euphemisms disappear with George Michael's brazen declaration, "I Want Your Sex."
- 1991—Color Me Badd crudely and unflinchingly declares, "I Wanna Sex You Up."
- 1994—Exactly 30 years after the Beatles first proposed hand-holding, rapper R. Kelly scores a best-selling single with the sexually descriptive ode to intercourse, "Bump & Grind."[11]

Perhaps most disturbing of all is that rock fans not only accept the graphic references to sex in the lyrics of their favorite songs, they've come to expect them. Many defend such lyrics "on principle." Bob Smithouser and Bob Waliszewski, editors of Focus on the Family's *Plugged In,* a monthly publication devoted to analyses of current trends in pop culture, report that many teens, including some who attend church and call themselves Christians, object vociferously to critical reviews of violent and/or sexually explicit CDs and music videos.

Why? Because, as they see it, the music is simply a reflection of "real life." "Music and spiritual beliefs are two different things," wrote a girl named Sarah. "Sex, drugs, alcohol—those things are all found in more places than in music. It is *reality.*"[12] That in itself is a revealing commentary on the world in which we live.

Apparently Matt and Jack are right. Unless you're willing to cut yourself off completely from television, rock music, radio, and the other mass media, it's practically impossible to escape the message that sex—as much of it as you can get and with as many partners as possible—is what life is all about.

Drugs and Alcohol

> *I am extremely vulnerable when alcohol is involved....When the opposite sex is present and alcohol is involved—now that's the most frightening thing, because I really, really lack self-control, especially when I have been drinking.*
>
> —Mark (15)

> *Drugs and alcohol do add to making one more vulnerable.... Talking to some of my friends, I found that they have done some really stupid and some almost nefarious things involving sex because they were just not aware of what they were doing at the time. And they've admitted how stupid it was—what a mistake it was.*
>
> —Jack (18)

People do things when they're drunk or high that they wouldn't normally do. Moral principles and common sense tend to melt under the influence of alcohol. Even in very small amounts, alcohol works to soften up

that part of the brain that controls our inhibitions—those natural restraints that keep our
passions and emotions in check and hold us
back from doing what we know in our hearts
is wrong or dangerous or unwise.

Alcohol is insidious and deceptive. It
gives the drinker a false sense of well-being
while numbing the intellect and slowing
down normal reflexes and bodily functions.
And if you don't happen to have any strong
principles or inhibitions in the first place, it's a
toss-up what you'll do when confronted with
an opportunity to take advantage of another
person sexually—or to sell yourself cheap.

"Drugs and alcohol are having a devastating effect on teen sexuality," says Michelle
Baranek. Michelle has seen and heard just
about everything imaginable in her work
with kids. "In the majority of date rape situations both the victim and the perpetrator
have been drinking," she says. "I used to be a
rape counselor, and a number of the young
ladies I've counseled were raped while
under the influence of alcohol."

One study indicated that 60 percent of
college women newly diagnosed with a sexually transmitted disease were drunk at the
time of infection. Furthermore, 90 percent of
rapes that occur on campus happen when
alcohol is used.[13]

Author Robin Warshaw breaks it down this way: 56 percent of teen girls who are raped are raped by a date; 30 percent are raped by a friend; 11 percent are raped by a boyfriend; and of all these so-called "acquaintance rapes," *90 percent* involve alcohol. And then consider that alcohol has been shown to be a factor in 100 percent of gang rapes.[14]

The frightening thing is that some people have been led to believe that drugs and alcohol act as a kind of aphrodisiac. In other words, they've been told that a drink or two can improve their love life. "There's a myth in our society," Michelle continues, "that says drugs and alcohol 'get you in the mood'—especially alcohol. That's not true. They lower your standards so that you're not able to make good decisions."

And the results of those poor decisions won't go away with the hangover. They're permanent.

◎   ◎   ◎

What now? thought Steve. For the space of maybe half a minute he sat staring at the darkened street outside the coffee shop window, barely aware of the struggle taking shape within him.

The Sarah who had draped herself over his shoulder was a Sarah he'd never known.

He'd always thought of pretty, blonde Sarah as fun and cute—even a bit childlike. In fact, turning it over in his mind, he realized that her childlikeness was one of the things that had made her so attractive to him in the first place.

But if she'd been attractive in the past, she was alluring now. Powerfully. The softness of her cheek against his, her satiny fingers on his neck, her hand taking liberties with his hair—taken together, it all exerted an overwhelming effect on him.

There could be no mistaking her meaning. Parents not home. A bottle of vodka. A not-so-subtle suggestion that they forget the basketball game and change their plans. He wouldn't have expected any of this from her. He'd been caught off balance. And somewhere inside his head he heard a tiny voice saying, *Maybe I should go for it.*

Not that he'd never pictured himself having sex with Sarah. Images like that have a way of crossing a guy's mind uninvited. But tonight it was more than a fanciful idea; it was a real possibility. A likelihood, even. It could happen. And why not? He had friends who were doing it—friends who actually bragged about doing it. *She's never thrown herself at me—or anyone else—like this before,* he thought. *Some guys would give blood for this kind of "opportunity."*

"Sarah," he said, turning his head to look into her eyes. His heart was pounding so that he could hardly speak.

"What, Stevie?"

The reek of alcohol on her breath struck him full in the face, and it was as if he'd been doused with a bucket of cold water. All at once he realized that this new Sarah, this provocative, suggestive, aggressive Sarah, was making him terribly uncomfortable. Sudden fear and a sense of strangeness overcame every other sensation. And in the next instant it all came back to him.

He'd been over this ground before! He remembered now—vaguely, and as if viewing it all through a tunnel, but still with a growing conviction that somewhere, in some previous life, before her hands had begun caressing his neck in just this way, he had already reached a decision.

What was it? *Save sex for marriage...*right?

Yes—the smell of the vodka had removed all doubt. The spell was broken, and he knew for a fact that jumping into bed with Sarah would be the same as strolling off a third floor ledge. How in the world could he have forgotten so quickly?

"Sarah," he repeated in a firmer, steadier voice.

"Hmm?"

"Let's just go to the game. Okay?"

"Okay," she said, unwinding her arms from around his neck and stumbling backward. "Whatever...."

When Steve closed his eyes later that night, alone in his own bedroom, it was with a sense of accomplishment. The temptation had been right there. So had the opportunity. It would have been so easy. But he'd made the right choice—for himself, and for Sarah. And now he felt just a little bit stronger.

The word was on his lips as he fell asleep. *Stronger.*

3

Falling Into
the Gap

Leslie was looking for a hug.
She came from a home where people
didn't express love physically; where no one
ever put an arm around her, drew her close,
or touched her affectionately; where no one
bothered to say, "I love you—you have value,
you have worth." Leslie doesn't remember
getting a hug from her parents until she had
reached her twenties.

A slim, brown-eyed brunette in her junior
year, Leslie was a lot like most other middle-
class, Midwestern high school girls: busy
with school, cheerleading, friends, and
extracurricular activities. A typical teen of the
late '60s and early '70s, she loved the colorful

and daring fashions of the time—mini-skirts, bell-bottoms, hip-huggers—and had a penchant for anything out of the ordinary. But she took her studies seriously and fully intended to go to college someday.

Bouncy and vivacious, well-liked on campus, funny, fun-loving, and famous for her wild, infectious laugh, Leslie thrived on the high school experience, both academically and socially. She absolutely loved it.

Perhaps she liked school so much because it made up for other things—important things noticeably lacking in her home. For Leslie, life at home was less than ideal. Her family would have received failing marks in Expressing Support and Demonstrating Affection. Her mom worked outside of the home and struggled with alcoholism and other issues of her own. Short on patience, she seldom felt inclined to spend much time with her four daughters. Leslie's dad was frequently away on military assignments. For Leslie, these absences were a welcome relief from the times he was at home—times she remembers as filled with her dad's verbal abuse of the family, intensified by his own struggle with alcohol. And Leslie? She was neither the smartest nor the prettiest nor the most talented child in a family where brains, looks, and ability were generally considered the most reliable measures of human worth.

Leslie's three sisters used to say she was just a little crazy. She didn't really object—she enjoyed being an eccentric—although sometimes the feeling that she was "different" or the "runt of the litter" left her with a sense of rejection. Of all the daughters, she was most likely to be picked on or made the butt of jokes. But that was okay. She had discovered ways of coping with her particular set of personal pressures and disappointments and knew how to have a good time despite them all.

But still…she knew something was missing. Leslie wanted—more desperately than she'd ever realized—to know what it felt like to be loved. To her lifelong sorrow, she found someone more than willing to accommodate her.

"I could have said no and let him walk away," she says, "and I would have had a completely different life." But her feeling of need seemed so strong. She was desperate for a hug.

When she found it, it came from a guy who looked for all the world like the perfect steady boyfriend. "I had dated a few other boys, one time here, two times there, but I think I was a little too goofy for them. This guy seemed to like the same kinds of things I liked. He seemed to like school." They started dating, and the relationship progressed rapidly.

At first it seemed too good to be true, all fun and laughter. Dates, dances, parties, and football games. And through it all the warm glow—the pleasure and satisfaction of being seen on the arm of a handsome guy. But all too abruptly, the relationship took an unexpected turn.

"About two months along, he began pressuring me for more than just a date. He started expecting me to spend less time with my friends and more time with him, more time after dark, more time away from my home and the surroundings that were comfortable to me. He began touching me way too much, way too fast.

"When I think back, the kinds of things he would say to me were extremely manipulative. Things like: 'You're the person I've been waiting for my whole life'; and 'I know we were made for each other. It's too bad we're so young—we're really ready to get on with our lives'; and 'I love you. I know you love me. The right thing to do, really, is to become very physical.' He told me how neat I was, how funny I was, how he thought I was pretty. Things I never heard in my home."

Eventually, it happened. And trauma

struck. For Leslie, that first attempt at intercourse could be described only as a nightmare. And not because of faulty expectations;
she never had any. She had been too ignorant
to know what to expect.

So great was the shock, the discomfort,
and the sense of loss, that Leslie was ready to
put on the brakes—and fast. For her, that first
sexual encounter served as a rude wake-up
call. All she longed for now was to return to
the time of innocence. "I didn't want to go
through this again. I wanted to go back to
hand-holding and kissing. Couldn't we just
go back to that? But that was not what this
young man had in mind."

Far from it. As far as *he* was concerned,
the fun was just beginning. Sex was what he
had been aiming at from the start, and now
that he'd made his first conquest, he wasn't
about to forfeit the advantage. So sex became
the central theme, almost the purpose, of the
relationship.

"He begged me constantly: 'Can we have
sex tonight? Can we get together? I want to
touch you. I want to be with you.' It was a constant part of every conversation. There was no
more talk about friends or parties or football
games. It was all about us, alone in a room by
ourselves, going further than I wanted to go."

And somehow, she felt she *couldn't* say no.

She was afraid of how he might react if she turned him off. "If you want me to stay as your boyfriend," he'd say, "you'll continue to be this way with me." And she needed his "love" too much to refuse. To say no would have been too risky. Or so it seemed at the time.

◎　◎　◎

Looking for Answers

Where are teens when it comes to sex today? In some ways, it's a mixed bag. The range of kids' thoughts, feelings, and opinions on the subject seems as wide and multicolored as a cathedral-sized mosaic. But like any mosaic, this patchwork of opinion and attitude is best viewed from a distance. Step back, get some perspective, and you'll see patterns begin to emerge. Here are some basic figures that help to give the picture some clarity:

- By their fifteenth birthday, 10 percent of girls and 27 percent of boys have had sexual intercourse; by age 18, the numbers rise to 56 percent for females and 73 percent for males.[1]
- This indicates a rise in sexual activity among teens since the early 1970s, when the figures for 18-year-olds were 35 percent for young women and 55 percent for young men.[2]

- *On the other hand,* some of the most recent studies of sexual behavior among teens have suggested that as of 1995, a growing percentage of 15- to 19-year-olds was refraining from initiating sexual activity.[3]
- The likelihood of engaging in intercourse increases steadily with age: from 16 percent at age 13, to 42 percent at age 16, to 71 percent at age 18.[4]
- The average age of first sexual intercourse is 17 for females and 16 for males.[5]
- Teens who engage in other risky behaviors, such as drug use, are more likely to have sex at younger ages.[6]
- Roughly 50 percent of high school students have not had sex, and of those who have had intercourse at least one time, at least 25 percent have not had sex within the past three months.[7]
- Seven in 10 women who had sex before age 14, and 6 in 10 of those who had sex before age 15, report having had sex involuntarily.[8]

On the whole, today's teens are far more likely to engage in premarital sexual experimentation than their grandparents and great-grandparents. But they also seem to be re-evaluating the principles of "sexual liberation" that were introduced by their parents' generation. Generally speaking, this is a picture of a generation in flux—a group of people who are a little confused, but open-minded and honestly seeking.

To indulge or not to indulge? To abstain or not to abstain? Teens today genuinely want to know, and they aren't necessarily taking *anybody* else's word for it. They want solid, reliable, satisfactory answers to their questions.

This is a day of free and easy attitudes toward sex. And there are plenty of people of all ages who think this is a good thing. Why, they ask, should something as natural and normal as sex be turned into a cause of so much confusion and controversy and personal pain?

Mike and Eva Ashburn have heard it all. All the arguments. All the tired lines. All the justifications. But they have also been up close and personal with those who have lived through the dark side of sexual "freedom."

Mike is the special assistant to the president for Young Life, a highly respected Christian youth ministry organization. As speakers, entertainers, and representatives-at-large for Young Life, Mike and his wife

Eva have spent the past couple of decades talking with teens about sex. They conduct seminars on the subject in a wide variety of settings and venues—everywhere from living rooms to convention centers—all across the country. And they know that, despite the cheerful confidence with which some kids refer to the advantages of today's relaxed sexual standards, many sexually active teens are hurting badly. Mike and Eva have seen the look of pain and doubt in the eyes of the young people who come to them for advice. They hear it in their voices. They've traced the evidence of it in their lives.

Mike (better known to his friends as "Ash") sums it up by saying, "I believe that sexuality is the number one topic kids are struggling with today."

Tug-of-War

So what's the struggle all about?

Picture a piece of rope in a tug-of-war. One team pulls in one direction while their opponents yank as hard as they can in the other. This way and that way, back and forth—the harder the tussle, the greater the tension on the fibers of the cord. Sooner or later one side gives way to the other. Or something snaps.

Teenagers today are like that piece of

rope—caught somewhere between the poles of two opposing forces, two competing ideas.

On the one hand, they hear constantly that sex is a great thing. Long gone are the days of Victorian taboos, when talk of sex was forbidden. Nowadays, it's openly discussed almost everywhere. Rock videos habitually include subtle and not-so-subtle references to and depictions of the sex act. Kids talk sex in the locker rooms, in the hallways, and in the classroom. Movies and television glorify it. Advertising swims in it. It's everywhere—like a national religion.

But kids are also being told, by a number of authorities and for a variety of reasons, to leave sex alone—at least for the time being. They've heard that the wonders and pleasures of sex are accompanied by grave dangers, or that it's wrong or unwise to indulge sexual desire until certain prerequisites have been met.

If you're old enough and physically mature enough to be sexually awake and aware, you're feeling the tension. You're being pulled in two directions at the same time.

Sex Is Good . . .

The message I would love for teenagers to hear more than any

*other is that God is the author
and perfecter of sex.*
—Mike Ashburn

Let's take a closer look at the opposing forces competing in this tug-of-war. At one end of the rope is the idea that sex is good, a beautiful part of what it means to be a man or a woman.

"Sexuality is a wonderful, God-given gift," says Ash. "I think God loves sex. That's an idea that takes kids by surprise. They've been inundated with messages like, 'Hey, don't do it! Sex is wrong and terrible.' But God is the author and perfecter of sex. From the very beginning, male and female were created for sexual love with each other. And God gives us the parameters that make it perfect: the confines of a marriage relationship."

We were made to find fulfillment through this kind of whole-person communication and interaction. Our bodies, minds, and emotions are designed, among other things, to function sexually. And when it's time to begin shifting into that mode—for most of us, at some point during the teen years—the body's endocrine system lets us know in no uncertain terms by releasing a flood of powerful sex-related hormones into the bloodstream.

Everyone feels the effect—intensely. Let's face it: Once past the age of puberty, we all begin to take a lively interest in sex.

"God beautifully designed the sexes for one another," writes Dr. James Dobson in *Life on the Edge*, "giving each gender the precise characteristics needed by the other. Consider, for example, how men and women's bodies were crafted to 'fit' together sexually. Anyone, even the most avid evolutionist, can see that they were constructed anatomically for one another. In the same way, the emotional apparatus of males and females is designed to interlock. It fits like hand in glove."[9]

So sex is a good thing. A desirable thing. Everybody feels it and everybody wants it—especially when the streams of sex-related hormones and sexual maturity are just beginning to flow. It's part of the Creator's perfect design for human life.

"God created sexual passion," says author Steve Arterburn. "If He would have been interested only in propagation, He could have designed a baby button, and the husband could have turned it on at night like he might a light switch. But sex, in God's wonderful and creative design, is to be more than just a way to make babies. It is a phenomenal way of showing love and intimacy with another person. The two shall become one."[10]

And that, as far as it goes, is exciting news.

... But Not Right Now

The other pole of the tug-of-war over sex has to do with timing, readiness, and (to use the current term) "safety." Sex is *such* a good thing, such a sacred, holy, perfectly designed, and powerful thing, that it *has* to be kept for the proper time and place. Otherwise its goodness is lost or spoiled or destroyed.

And that's not all. If sexual desires are indulged in the wrong way or outside the proper context, the side effects can be disastrous—sometimes even fatal. In some ways (believe it or not), sex is like reading: It's good, fun, and adds to our enjoyment of life—but done in the wrong context, it can be destructive. Would you like to travel down a superhighway filled with drivers immersed in a John Grisham novel? I wouldn't. Reading is good, but not while you're driving— unless you want to get acquainted with an ambulance . . . or a hearse.

There are many reasons to *wait* for sex, and they're all worth serious consideration. We'll take a closer look at them in later chapters, but here are just a few thoughts to bear in mind for the time being:

- Sex is more fulfilling and satisfying when enjoyed within marriage.
- Married people who have saved themselves for one another sexually are generally healthier, happier, and more secure than those who have not.
- Sex outside of marriage is risky: Unwanted pregnancy, sexually transmitted diseases, and the possibility of future infertility are constant dangers.
- Premarital sex can distort or destroy an otherwise healthy relationship.
- Sex before marriage often impairs an individual's ability to function successfully within marriage later in life.

The Longing for Permanence

"Sex," says Eva Ashburn, "is about commitment and endurance and longevity." She's right. That's why the best place for sexual activity is within a permanent relationship between two people who are ready, willing, and able to give themselves to one another, body and soul, for "as long as they both shall live." Romance, sex, and marriage really do belong together. The old schoolyard sing-song had it right: "First comes love, then comes marriage, then comes a baby in the baby carriage."

To a certain extent, this basic truth is an important part of the sexual tension teens feel today. We can deny it, of course. We can talk about "sexual liberation" as much as we like. But in our heart of hearts, many of us can't escape a nagging feeling that sex should be reserved for a *permanent* relationship (this intuition can be especially strong in girls). That's one reason sexually active teens end up so painfully at odds with themselves.

You may disagree with that last point, but stop and think about it for a moment. When the average guy or girl "falls in love," aren't his or her feelings for the Beloved usually marked by an almost painful longing for *permanence*? How else do you explain the hundreds of love songs that contain lines like "I'm gonna love you till the stars fall from the sky," or "I know this love of mine will never die," or "We'll be together forever, until the end of time"? Such language comes naturally to lovers. That's why the updated and edited vows you can hear at some "trendy" and "progressive" weddings these days seem to fall so flat: "I promise to love you until life's diverging pathways lead us in different directions." That's no promise at all.

What if Romeo and Juliet had talked that way? Shakespeare's famous play would be transformed from a tragedy into a comedy! There's a reason why we've come to think of *Romeo and Juliet* as the "ultimate love story": The hero and heroine symbolize for us the unshakable loyalty and commitment—even to the point of death—of *true* lovers. That's what sexual attraction, sexual activity, sexual bonding, and marriage are all about. And that's why it's so important, hard though it may seem, to *wait* until we can get them in a single package.

"When you're having sex with someone," says Leslie, "you're making a decision—'this could be my partner for life.'" With all her heart, she wishes she'd realized that *then,* instead of now.

"I don't think a lot of teens know about the emotional side of sex until they experience it," says Jack. "I didn't know about it until I lost my virginity." Even when you're not expecting it, sex, like emotional super glue, has a way of tying you to another person. Jack's heart was telling him what his head and his hormones had forgotten to mention: "You should have waited."

Aggravating Times,
Aggravating Circumstances

Teens face a lot of tension and stress on the sexual side of life. "Sex is good—but you'll have to wait to enjoy it." Young people probably have been caught up in this frustrating dilemma since the beginning of human history. But there *are* some things about our times that aggravate the tension and increase the intensity of the tug-of-war.

We can describe the sexual pressures today's teens are facing in terms of three "gaps"; three points of frustration unique to Western culture as we enter a new millennium; three places where contemporary kids run up against unbridged chasms between urgent sexual desire and a reasonable willingness to put it on hold. We'll call them the Hormone Gap, the Morality Gap, and the Love and Marriage Gap.

"The Hormone Gap"

The first gap has to do with *time*. It's the gap of an extended waiting period. Eighteen-year-old Jack makes an interesting observation: "A long time ago, people got married really young, and then they had children. But that doesn't happen anymore because society has changed."

Jack has put his finger on something.

Those clashing messages—"Sex is something worth having *now*!" and "Sex should be *saved* for marriage"—come into even sharper conflict when we shove the possibility of marriage into a far-distant future. After high school. After college. After careers begin.

After, after, after.

That, in a sense, is exactly what the modern social structure has done. It really *was* different in the "olden days." A boy became a man as soon as he could follow the plow, and society determined a girl's womanhood by her physical ability to bear children. These days, the push to get a college education, the practical necessity of pinning down and following career goals, and the financial challenges that come with the package have removed marriage far beyond the reach of adolescents. Social pressures and economics have put permanent, committed love in the "out-of-the-question" category for teens—at the very time when their hormones begin to rage!

It can even be argued that "teenagers"— people in adult bodies who aren't yet ready to live adult lives—are a relatively recent invention. In past generations, lots of couples became full-fledged adults and entered into wedlock before reaching the age of 20. Today the average male won't start thinking seriously about marriage until he's close to 26.

Meanwhile, nothing has happened to prevent young adults from feeling their sexual "oats." Those natural, normal sexual urges are as real and present as ever. There is even evidence to suggest that they are making themselves felt at an earlier age with every passing generation. In other words, kids are maturing faster these days. In the United States the average age of first menstruation in girls dropped from 16.5 in 1840 to 12.9 in 1950.[11]

Dr. Neil Clark Warren, counselor, writer, and widely respected expert on marriage, believes that the pressures of modern life require young people to take longer to prepare themselves for marriage than in the past. "In this particular time," he says, "when people are taking longer for education and when they are buffeted by so many more stimuli from television and movies—when it's harder and more complicated getting to know yourself—I suggest that they wait a little longer before making a decision to marry." Dr. Warren says the strongest modern marriages result when both partners wait until about age 28 before tying the knot. But he also admits that things were different in simpler times: "My mother was 17 and my dad was 19 when they got married. Their marriage lasted for almost 71 years, and they were extremely happy."[12]

In *Life on the Edge*, Dr. James Dobson calls the years between ages 16 and 26 "the critical decade"—the 10 years during which young people must face and answer hundreds of important questions about their lives and personal destinies. One of them is the question of how to handle the sexual drive. It's ironic that those same 10 years roughly parallel the "waiting period" between puberty and what modern society considers "marriageable age."

This is the "hormone gap"—the delay between the awakening of sexual desire and the opportunity to fulfill it in its proper setting. In many ways, it's unique to our era. And there's no denying it: It isn't an easy stretch of life to navigate.

Ten years is a long time. Ten *days* seem like a long time when you're a kid. No wonder teens today feel stretched and stressed. "Abstain until I'm married?" asks Jack. "I'd have to say that I disagree. Because I find that nowadays no one really wants to stick to that ... unless, of course, they're very religious."

Go back to Romeo and Juliet for just a moment. They were probably about 15 and 17 years old (maybe even younger!) when they met at a masked ball and fell hopelessly in love. Then what did they do? Start looking for a motel room? No—they sneaked off to Friar Lawrence to be secretly *married*. It wasn't their *youth* that made this marriage so unthinkable—people their age got married all the time back in the fifteenth century. The difficulty in this case was that their families hated each other. But suppose the venerable father, when they came to him to have the knot tied, had said, "Sorry, kids, but I can't possibly marry you now. You won't be finished with your master's degrees for at least another six years!" What do you think the two impassioned lovers would have done at *that* point?

"The Morality Gap"

The second gap—the Morality Gap—concerns *confused standards*. It's the place where teens fall into the ditch of sexual temptation because they really aren't sure what to think about right and wrong.

Another thing our grandparents and great-grandparents had going for them was a strong set of moral guidelines regarding sex and marriage: ground rules that everybody more or less took for granted and never thought about questioning (even when they were breaking them). It's different now. Today, our society expects teens to make up their own guidelines and chart their own unique course through the jungle of love and relationships.

That may sound great to some of us, like an invitation to total freedom. But the responsibility of blazing your own trail through the wilderness of romance and sex is a heavy burden to bear. This so-called "freedom" is the reason for a great deal of confusion that surrounds the subject today. A man traversing the Amazon rain forest without map or compass wouldn't feel liberated. He'd just feel lost.

"Kids *are* looking for guidelines," says Mike Ashburn. "They're asking, 'Give me some parameters I can live with in this area and still be pleasing to God.'" And the sad thing is, it's becoming harder and harder to find adults who are willing to give them the answers they're seeking.

Maybe that's why 16-year-old Joseph feels so strongly that "teens today are lost." He's watched his friends wander around inside this huge "morality gap" and he's seen how much it hurts when they stumble and fall.

"The Love and Marriage Gap"

The last gap—the Love and Marriage Gap—has to do with *lost hope*. It's the gap that opens when waiting seems useless;

when you reach the conclusion that the idea of finding satisfying sex within a loving marriage is just a cruel fantasy (and therefore decide to settle for something less).

We've argued that sex should be saved until it can be savored within the warmth and security of a lifelong marriage, that sex and permanent love belong together. Unfortunately, for many modern teens, this "permanent love requirement" has become another source of sexual tension and temptation. For them, it serves to split open another chasm between awakening sexual desire and any realistic expectation of fulfilling it in the best, most satisfying, and most "acceptable" way. This is because so many of us today have come to regard permanent love and a happy marriage as impossible dreams—prerequisites that can never be met.

And this is another point at which today's teens are confronted with a problem their grandparents and great-grandparents likely never faced. In the past, people were more hopeful about the possibility of finding faithful love *and* sexual fulfillment within *marriage.* In a way, it was easier for them to hold off on having sex because they took it for granted that "their time was coming."

But what happens when you become convinced there is no such thing as lifelong love, and that you'll never be able to find it no matter how hard you try? You've heard that sex is for marriage; okay, fine. But what if all the evidence seems to indicate that marriage is terribly painful and disappointing—something to be avoided at all costs?

That conviction can destroy hope. Unfortunately, it doesn't take away desire.

It's like being told that you can have your dessert—just as soon as you find the Holy Grail or discover a cure for cancer. When the bar is set *that* high, pressure to ignore the requirements and take a quick shortcut to immediate gratification can become irresistible.

Josh McDowell, for more than three decades a highly effective communicator of biblical truths and successful life principles to America's teenagers, says that kids today are hurting badly. According to his statistics, 37 percent of adolescents contemplate suicide, and eight out of 100 actually attempt it. Why? Josh thinks he has an answer.

"The two greatest fears that motivate young people today," he says, "are (1) the fear that I'll never be loved; and (2) the fear that I'll never be able to love. God intended that we should learn how to love by seeing our fathers love our mothers. When you break down that model in the home, you end up with a generation that doesn't know how to give or receive love."

Today, statistics indicate that one out of every two marriages—a full 50 percent!—will eventually end in divorce, many of them within the first five years. No wonder a lot of kids are skeptical! No wonder they feel that sexual pleasure is beyond reach if it can *only* be enjoyed within the context of permanent, marital love. Under the circumstances, it's easy for them to interpret the traditional insistence on keeping sex and marriage together as unreasonable and unfair. Even cruel and inhuman. They've seen too many failures, too many cases where love was promised but failed to materialize. As they see it, lasting love is an unachievable ideal.

This honest disillusionment about love and marriage tugs at the rope and further aggravates the tension today's teens feel concerning sexual desire. There's a strong temptation to leap the gap in a single bound, bypass all the pain, the hard work, and the long stretches of time required to grow true love, and simply jump into bed together *right now.*

◎　◎　◎

The day came when Leslie discovered she was pregnant. She told her mom; her mom cried and got angry. She told her dad; he cried too, and kept his distance (as always). She told her best friend, and *she* cried. She turned in her cheerleading uniform, and the head of the cheerleading squad cried. The tears flowed.

Funny thing was, everyone was crying—except Leslie. Somehow, her naturally buoyant personality and naïveté gave her a confidence that, despite rejection, anger, tears, and negative reactions, everything would turn out fine.

But something more than her natural optimism left her with such a hopeful outlook. Strange as it sounds, Leslie was pinning her hopes on *marriage.* She actually convinced herself that pregnancy was the best thing that could have happened to her. Not that she didn't have her fears and anxieties. But somehow she had got hold of the idea—or it had got hold of her—that this turn of events might be the insurance policy she'd been looking for all her life; that now the hugging and the loving and the feeling of belonging that she wanted so badly could never be taken away from her. Sex, pregnancy, marriage, and lifelong love—they just go together, right? It made sense to *her.*

I get to hold onto this guy forever now, she thought. *Now I'll have someone who really loves me.*

If only it had been that simple.

4

Before You Leap

Q: *Is it better to wait to have sex?*
Courtney: *That's personal business, but I think you ought to wait until some age.*
Q: *What age?*
Courtney: *Well, I don't know ... about 15, for example.*

Adrienne

At 15, Adrienne was an average, well-adjusted, all-American high school girl. For her, life was pretty simple—a question of keeping up with homework, having fun, and hanging out. Academically, she was a winner: a straight-A student enrolled in advanced-level courses. She had a talent for science, and some of her projects had gone all the way to national competitions. She came from a Christian home, enjoyed a supportive relationship with her family, had good looks, popularity, a crowd of friends, and involved herself in lots of extracurricular activities at school.

Adrienne took it all for granted. Little did she know that her life was about to turn a corner.

"I don't know if my decision to become sexually active was necessarily something that I sat down and thought about," says Adrienne. "It's not like I went over the consequences and issues in my head and then came to the conclusion that it was something I was going to do. It wasn't something that I had *decided*. I never said, 'Tonight I'm going to lose my virginity and become sexually active.' It was something that sort of happened to me."

It happened on the night of her 16th birthday. No one put on the pressure. He didn't force her and she didn't try to seduce him. When it happened, it happened because of fuzzy thinking and unquestioned assumptions.

"I guess I just figured this was kind of the next logical step in our relationship. We were convinced that we were going to get married one day, that we were just so much in love. I was the last one of all my friends to lose my virginity."

Today, Adrienne is living with her parents, trying to raise a toddler and finish school at the same time. She struggles a lot with loneliness. There's no time for friends or a social life.

"I think self-control is something I chose not to exercise when I was in high school," she says. "I wanted to have sex, so I did. There's been a lot of guilt associated with that decision."

Hear Adrienne's thoughts about life after turning that corner.

"I wish *every day of my life* that my virginity was something that I still had, that I had taken a stand to be abstinent, that the decision to have sex was a decision I still had to make. If I had to go back and do it all over again, I would definitely do things differently."

"It Just Sort of Happened"

Funny, isn't it? The situations you find yourself in when things just sort of *happen?* Situations you never once imagined in your wildest dreams or worst nightmares. You end up down a hard road in a strange place, wondering how you got there and where you missed the turn. You follow a feeling, yield to a momentary passion, and—just that quickly—everything changes. Forever.

It isn't at all like video games where you have seven lives and throw six of them away just to learn the course. This is the real thing. There's only one life. And there's no pushing a button that clears the screen and starts a new game. Too many people think about sex as something that "just happens when it happens." Something that takes you by surprise, catches you off-guard, or bursts upon you like a sudden storm when you're with the right person, or when opportunity and passion and overflowing hormones suddenly sweep you off your feet and carry you away like a riptide. It's natural. It's normal. It feels good. Why spoil it by asking too many questions? I'll deal with the consequences later.

So many teens could echo Adrienne's story. Over and over again you hear phrases like …

"I never really thought much about it."

"It just sort of happened."

"I didn't have a clue what was going on."

"I never imagined that things would turn out this way."

You can't help wondering how many of these same people would slide into the driver's seat of their parents' car for the first time "without really thinking about it" (but then, maybe some would!). Or how many of them just "happened" to get a passing grade on an important geometry test. Can you—on an impulse—walk into an eye surgeon's office and submit to radial keratotomy, allowing the surgeon to peel back your cornea with a laser? It isn't something you jump into without giving it some thought—without understanding some of the risks. Most of us wouldn't even buy a pair of shoes without shopping around, checking quality, comparing prices, and deciding whether the merchandise was worth the cost.

Why is it that decisions about sexual activity—a thing so deeply rooted in our humanity that it has the power to impact our lives and the lives of others in drastic and permanent ways—get so little thought? Why do we so seldom stop to ponder the implications? It's almost unbelievable how, when it comes to sex, so many kids today leap before they look.

Unconcerned

Unfortunately, it's not just teens who seem unconcerned about the wider implications of sexual activity outside of marriage. A lot of people—smart, educated, successful people — turn out to be clueless when making responsible choices about sex. It's a sign of the times.

Take professional athletes, for example. We look up to them as heroes and role models.

They enjoy money, visibility, and prestige, and live the kinds of lives most of us can only dream about. And what are they doing with all that power and popularity? Apparently some of them are indulging in a lot of thoughtless and irresponsible sex—and fathering a daunting number of illegitimate children as a result. At least that's the story we get from a recent *Sports Illustrated* article.

That article examined the "flip attitude toward unplanned fatherhood" that seems commonplace in the world of professional sports. Speaking about the National Basketball Association, ESPN broadcaster and former NBA player and agent Len Elmore said, "I would guess that one [out-of-wedlock child] for every player is a good ballpark figure. For every player with none, there's a guy with two or three." Elmore went on to comment, "Today's athletes just don't care. They're hung up on instant gratification. There's no view of the impact that present-day decisions have on the future."[1]

Instant gratification. A "flip" attitude. No concern for future consequences. These are some of the worst sex-related diseases in the world. They're diseases of the heart and mind, and they're afflicting increasing numbers of people, young and old, in our generation—people who say, "Hey, sex is for fun; I'll take my fun wherever and whenever I happen to find it, and I don't care who I may hurt in the process."

Sarah

Sarah's another example of a girl who didn't have a clue. That's not to say she was dumb. On the contrary, Sarah was very bright, blessed with a healthy share of positive qualities and winsome traits. Picture her as tall and blonde, with warm, expressive blue eyes; the kind of girl who is pretty in a very simple and natural way; gentle, sensitive, and soft-spoken. Responsible and self-motivated, she took the initiative to cover some of her own school expenses by working a part-time job after school. She was also a Christian—believed in the Bible, had strong feelings about the immorality of abortion, and thought it was wrong to have sex before marriage.

Sarah met Jimmy at the local Taco Bell, where they both held after-school jobs. Jimmy came from Honduras. She didn't know it, but he was an unregistered alien, working illegally in the United States. A couple of other things she didn't know about: his short-fused temper and tendency to act out his frustrations and aggressions. Those aspects of his personality stayed conveniently hidden during those early days under a sparkling layer of boyish charm.

As the months passed, Jimmy and Sarah spent a lot of time together behind the counter at Taco Bell. It wasn't long before they found familiarity turning to attraction. And attraction giving way to passion.

"I guess we just clicked somehow," Sarah says. "Things proceeded from there."

Was it love?

"I thought so," she recalls. "I did think that I was in love. When I was having sex with him, there was a feeling that this is what love is supposed to be like. But looking back, I realize it was lust—just the feeling of what I was feeling."

And so, as Sarah puts it, things proceeded from there—on the basis of a "feeling about a feeling." They proceeded from attraction to passion, from feelings to actions, from a first-time encounter to an increasingly complicated series of events—a whole new pattern of behavior in which physical pleasure somehow got the upper hand.

Sarah and Jimmy had crossed a line: Sex—in regular doses—had become an indispensable and inevitable part of their relationship.

Birth control? Not for Sarah. The thought that she might possibly want to take precautions against an unwanted pregnancy never occurred to her. Besides, she wouldn't even *think* of asking her parents to take her to the doctor for contraceptives. And despite all the highly publicized hype about condoms, Jimmy never used them. In fact, she never encouraged him to use them.

Why not?

"I knew I was having sex, but I didn't think that I could get pregnant. Sure, I'd go to class and they'd teach me about sex education and all that, but I think I just had the mindset that this only happens to a certain few people, that it wasn't going to happen to me. A lot of my friends did it, and none of them got pregnant, so . . ."

The Invincible "I"

Sex . . . without contraception? And no possibility of getting pregnant? How could anyone be so naive? Sarah gives us an important clue when she says, "I had the mindset that it wasn't going to happen to me."

Believe it or not, it's a common illusion. A sense of invulnerability and immortality often goes hand-in-hand with youth, health, strength, and energy. It leads some teenagers to take all kinds of unnecessary risks. It's something like the feeling that overwhelmed Master Colin in Frances Hodgson Burnett's famous story *The Secret Garden*. After experiencing the thrill of walking and running on his own two feet for the very first time, Colin exclaimed, "I'm going to live forever!"

When you feel as if you're going to live forever, there's no reason to be careful or worry about consequences. For the invulnerable, the world is just one great big roller coaster ride, and the scarier the better. So drive fast, forget the seatbelt, flirt with danger. After all, it's just for fun. *You* won't be the one to crash—or conceive a child. HIV, AIDS, chlamydia, gonorrhea? Illness, pain, sterility, death? That's stuff that happens to other people. Just a bunch of statistics in a health text.

We'll revisit this notion of the "Invincible 'I'" in a later chapter—when we discuss in depth the various risks associated with sexual activity outside of marriage. For now it's enough to note that, as in Sarah's case, feelings of invulnerability can foreshadow unexpected tragedy.

Get a Clue

> *I'm recommending that you think carefully, long and hard, before you enter a sexual relationship.*
> —Joanna Thompson
> National Coordinator, Care
> for the Family, U.K.

Nobody starts out on a long or difficult journey—a cross-country bike trip, for example, or a backpacking trek through the Sierras—without taking a good, long look at the map. Contractors don't turn a single shovelful of dirt or pound a single nail until they've first put a lot of time into studying their blueprints. And if you're thinking of spending the summer vacationing on the French Riviera, you'd better be sure you have a bank account back home hefty enough to cover the expense.

People who head off into the unknown without a plan end up in all kinds of unexpected trouble. The bigger the venture, the higher the stakes. The higher the stakes, the greater the risk. You'd better not take your life in your hands without a pretty good reason.

Social workers in the big cities run into this sort of thing all the time. A former director of the Deacon's Cupboard, a ministry supplying food and clothing to the homeless and needy at a large church in Los Angeles, says she constantly found herself engaged in conversations like the following with her clients:

Director: *Where are you staying now?*
Client: *In my car. Under the freeway near Franklin and Gower. With my wife and two kids.*

Director: *How long have you been there?*
Client: *We got into town last week. It's just temporary, until we can find something else.*
Director: *Did you have anything in mind when you came to Los Angeles?*
Client: *Not really. We just climbed in the car back in Ohio and headed for California.*
Director: *What do you plan to do next?*
Client: *I don't know.*

That kind of thoughtlessness can end up costing a bundle. The streets of downtown Los Angeles aren't a safe or comfortable place to live—even for a little while. And in the same way, an unplanned pregnancy, a premature and mismatched marriage, or a sexually transmitted disease can take more out of you than you ever thought possible. The results can be permanent—and, in some cases, devastating. It doesn't pay to let your brain take a back seat to your feelings and urges.

So get a clue—and get a plan. Despite everything you may have ever heard, read, assumed, or thought about it, sex is not merely a package of uncontrollable passions, unbridled feelings, and "free expression." Sex is, in fact, something that should unfold in each of our lives according to a careful and intentional design—a matter of thought, planning, choosing, deciding, and making a conscious commitment. It *can* be done. And it *should*...as Adrienne, Sarah, and Leslie will all tell you.

Leslie

Like Adrienne, Leslie never made a conscious decision to become sexually active. "It kind of snuck up on me," she says.

"I wish I'd been informed. I wish I'd understood what makes guys tick and what makes girls tick. I had no clue. I didn't realize that my boyfriend and I were on totally different planes, that there's something going on in the guy's mind. There was stuff going on in my mind, too—I mean, girls are full of hormones as well. But our hormones are thinking totally different things.

"Back then I had never really said the word 'sex' much. It was more like, 'Let's just give ourselves to each other.'"

And that's exactly what happened. Slowly at first, gradually, but surely and unmistakably.

"It was not a one-step thing. Little by little I'd give myself physically to this person. Little by little I began to give him my emotions. And then my personality left, and my circle of friends left, and pretty soon there wasn't anything left of *me*.

"I really didn't know what the natural progression was, so I never even thought about making a conscious decision to wait. Before I knew what I had done, I'd already given myself away to another person without realizing that I was supposed to wait for a special day to do that."

Then came the day when she found herself violently ill in the middle of a big cheerleading competition.

"That's when I found out I was pregnant," she remembers. "I thought I had the flu. I didn't even know how I got pregnant. There had been no concern about birth control, no concern over any of those issues. I really didn't think I could get pregnant. I'd only had my period for about nine or 10 months. I wasn't even regular. I really honestly didn't even think it was a possibility. And here I was, throwing up on a cheerleading competition weekend and discovering that my life was about to change."

That was more than 25 years ago. Leslie has traveled a long, hard road over the past two and a half decades: a baby out of wedlock, 10 years in a nightmarish marriage, physical and emotional abuse, thoughts of suicide, and the strain of raising two children on her own. But today the thing that hits her hardest about the loss of her virginity is that it happened out of thoughtlessness and ignorance.

"My biggest regret about my behavior back then is that I was totally clueless."

It doesn't have to be that way.

5

Risks

Philosophy was a difficult subject for Jeff. Difficult because it was dry and boring. Difficult because he couldn't see any point to it. Difficult because the print was so small in his Philosophy/English Lit textbook—two dreadful, long columns of text on every page, unbroken by anything except an occasional antique line drawing of some guy with a weird, unpronounceable name like Kierkegaard or Wittgenstein.

He was thumbing through that text now, cramming for the next morning's exam, anxiety and confusion and brain-numbness blocking out the rich smell of roasted espresso beans and the buzz of talk at the tables around him. Not his idea of a ripping good time.

In Kierkegaard's view, he read, *"existence" is to be contrasted with mere "life." True "existence" is achieved when one abandons the role of spectator and acts in accord with one's inner decisions. Meaningful "existence" is a matter of taking risks. The greater the value, the greater the risk.*

He sighed and looked up from the page, propping his chin in his hand. Just inside the entrance to the coffee shop, in a secluded space between a Japanese screen partition and a potted ficus tree, he caught sight of his friend Nate…standing nose to nose and hand in hand with Lisa Houghton. Nate was obviously under the girl's spell. Big time.

The two of them continued talking in animated whispers until Nate became aware of Jeff's incredulous stare. Holding up a finger as if to say, "Be with you in a minute," Nate turned back to Lisa for a few more minutes of talk and touching, then left her with a kiss on the lips.

"So what's with you and Lisa?" asked Jeff when Nate joined him at the table. "That was a pretty indiscreet little scene over there."

"What?" responded Nate with a *who, me?* look. "It's no big deal. She's just really friendly—if you know what I mean.…"

"Yeah, I know. I guess you and I have pretty different definitions of 'friendly.'"

"Friendly's friendly," said Nate, folding his arms across his chest and leaning back in his chair. "That doesn't bother me."

Jeff was turning over the pages of his philosophy text again. He shook his head and, without looking up, said in a lowered voice, "Lisa Houghton's only been with half the guys in this school. Do you think she's worth the risk?"

◎ ◎ ◎

Warning: Danger

I think sex is risky. There will always be a risk as long as you're having intercourse or any kind of sex.

—Jack (18)

I believe that love and marriage is the only bond strong enough to contain the sexual relationship.

—Michelle Baranek

Remember the question Jack raised in the last chapter? "I find a lot of adults saying, 'Don't have sex.' Since so many people say,

'Don't do it—you can't have that—,' it just makes you wonder, 'Why can't I? What will happen to me if I do?'"

In answer, let's first admit that sex pushes you into a zone of incredible risk. Thin ice. Walk on the cliff's edge. We're not just talking about the danger of getting caught, getting pregnant, or getting sick. Instead, we're referring to the nature of sex as an activity that touches and changes two people at virtually every level of their being.

The *risk* of sex isn't merely a question of a few minor traps and pitfalls that you avoid by "taking precautions."

That's the Big Lie floating around out there. In truth, the risk is bigger than that.

The danger goes deeper. Much deeper.

It has everything to do with the *power* and *mystery* of sex that we mentioned back in the first chapter: the inexplicable marvel of two people becoming one, physically, emotionally, and spiritually.

When you have sex with someone, you lay yourself open to that person. Like it or not, it's major surgery of the soul. You make yourself vulnerable, give yourself away. You don't leave the operating table as the same person you were when you were wheeled in. The potential results of sexual activity— namely, the formation of powerful emotional bonds and the possibility of conceiving children—have profound, far-reaching, even eternal implications.

That's why commitment, security, and permanence are so vital to a successful, meaningful, and satisfying sexual relationship. Sex, at the most fundamental level, boils down to a question of laying down your life for another person. And that's always risky.

Sex and Marriage

Wearing a condom during intercourse bears no resemblance to fastening your seat belt on a roller coaster. When you've been on a carnival ride, you climb out and say, "Wow. That was a rush. Where to now?" You've been engaged physically; you've experienced physical sensations. Then it's over.

Sex isn't like that. It isn't over when it's over. As someone has said, "They don't make a condom for the heart."

Or...do they?

Consider this: the danger of giving yourself away, body and soul, diminishes dramatically when the person on the other end of the transaction has promised to love, honor, and serve you "till death do you part." A vow like that, faithfully kept, makes all the difference in the world.

Sex *is* risky, but marriage is the safety net that makes the risk worth taking. It's the bond that preserves and protects. It's the place where interpersonal understanding has a chance to flower, where emotional bonds can grow deep and strong over time, and where a net of nurturing love can be spread to catch and hold any children that might happen to come along in the process. Marriage is the only thing strong enough to contain the power of sex and make it positive and constructive.

Really risky sex, then, is sex outside of marriage. That kind of sex is *very* dangerous—like walking on top of the handrail around the Grand Canyon. And the injuries you can inflict on yourself and others if you take that risk and fall are very real and specific. So let's get back to Jack's question: "What will happen to me" if I take the risk of engaging in sex outside the protective walls of marriage? Let's take a look at some of the possibilities.

Unwanted Pregnancy

> *Raising a child costs $474.00 a month. How much is your allowance?*
> —Message on a billboard

Remember Sarah? "I knew I was having sex," she said, "but I didn't think I could get pregnant ... I just had the mindset that this only happens to a certain few people, that it wasn't going to happen to me. A lot of my friends did it, and none of them got pregnant, so...."

Leslie, too, was shocked when intercourse led to pregnancy. "I really didn't think I could get pregnant," she said.

And Adrienne recalls, "On the night I lost my virginity I wasn't even thinking about birth control. I think that was the furthest thing from my mind."

All three girls ended up carrying and bearing unplanned babies. All three found out firsthand what it means to sacrifice youthful hopes and dreams to the unrelenting demands of motherhood. You would have thought that they'd have known better. You would have supposed that, with sex education and biology classes and all the information available to teens about sex today, they'd have made the logical connection. But a false sense of invincibility made them say, "It won't happen to *me*."

But it did. And it could happen to you, too.

It's time we all admitted it. If you're a sexually active female, you *can* get pregnant.

Not only *can* you get pregnant, there's a sense in which you're *supposed* to get pregnant. After all, that *is* an important part of the meaning and purpose of sex. "Before you enter into a sexual relationship," cautions Care for the Family's Joanna Thompson, "you need to realize that what you're doing is making a baby. You may use a contraceptive in the hope of preventing that, but nature has a wonderful way of overcoming obstacles. You might actually succeed in doing what we're created to do and made to do—which is to procreate."

And what if nature does succeed? A girl who becomes pregnant outside of marriage can deal with her situation in one of three ways. It's worth weighing the options before running the risk.

Option #1: Abortion

Pregnancy, of course, isn't the kind of consequence that stands alone. Pregnancy is just the beginning of other things. There are all kinds of ramifications and complications that come with it and grow out of it—choices, some of them difficult and agonizing, to be wrestled with and embraced.

Since abortion is legal in this country, the first decision a pregnant teen must make is whether she will deliver her baby. Many pregnant girls think of abortion as a simple, painless solution to an unlooked-for problem—girls like Adrienne.

"I didn't even consider any other options besides abortion," she says. "When I discovered I was pregnant for the first time, I decided that was what I had to do. As soon as I found out, I determined that I would abort the child. No one would ever have to know, I thought, and I could go on my merry way from there."

As it turned out, Adrienne's experience with abortion was anything but "merry." She went home that night and cried herself to sleep. To this day, years later, the loss of that child's life is a memory so painful she can't bear even to think about it.

That's the truth about abortion that often goes untold. Too many times the abortion debate gets reduced to nothing more than a battle of quick and easy bumper-sticker slogans. But no bumper sticker is big enough to contain even one of the stories of the thousands of women who live with regret every day of their lives because in a moment of fear and uncertainty they chose to destroy their own children.

Those feelings of regret can hit you years—even decades—after the fact. They can also begin in the abortion clinic itself.

One woman described her experience in the following terms: "I was taken into the recovery room, and all these girls were lying there on cots. They were all crying—the room was filled with their moans and groans. I thought, *If this is so right—if a woman should have the choice to kill the child in her womb—then why are we all crying about it? Why are we so upset about the choice we just made?*"[1]

If you're pregnant and unmarried, what you need to understand perhaps more than anything else is that abortion is an act of violence *against yourself.* That's not to minimize the fact that it also kills another human being. Anyone who thinks she can solve her own problems by terminating her baby's life is tragically deceived. But the point that often goes unmentioned is that abortion really does hurt women.

Think of it this way. Life with a child may be difficult and challenging, but it's also filled with thousands of precious moments and irreplaceable joys: the first tooth, the first word, the birthday cake on the baby's face, the funny things that only *your* boy or girl will think of saying.

Option #2: Raising the Child

For those who choose to carry their babies to term, another decision looms: to keep or not to keep the child? That's a weighty question for a 14-, 15-, or 16-year-old with no independent financial support. And it's an intimidating dilemma for a young woman with hopes, dreams, goals, and aspirations that don't necessarily include 2:00 A.M. feedings, diaper changes, and daycare. So what's a teenage mother to do? Keep her baby and scrap her plans for the future? Or give him up to be reared by someone else in order to stay on track with school or career? It's one of the most difficult decisions a person could ever be asked to make.

Sarah isn't sorry that she chose to keep *her* son. "I do regret having sex before I married," she says, "but that's not to say that I regret having my baby. My baby's the greatest thing I could ever ask for."

But what a price! Her life today is altogether different from the life she once pictured in her dreams. "There are things I can't do now that I wish I could do. Before having my baby, my dreams were to finish high school—which I didn't do—and go to college and become a child psychiatrist. But it's not like that now. I have my baby. I go to school—cosmetology school. It's not an ideal situation. Right now I'm planning to get my GED and eventually raise enough money doing cosmetology to put myself through college and still do what I want to do. But I could get stuck in cosmetology for the rest of my life. Not to say that's a bad thing. It's just … not what I wanted."

Option #3: Adoption

It's significant that not one of these girls opted to give up her child for adoption. That in itself says something about the power of maternal love. Not that adoption isn't a good idea. In many cases—perhaps most—it's the noblest, most loving thing an unmarried teenager can do for her child. It's a sacrificial gift that can bring a lifetime of happiness to some infertile married couple longing to hold a child of their own. And it gives the baby of a single mother the advantage of growing up in a two-parent home.

Joe White, director of the Kanakuk-Kanakomo Kamps and one of this country's most respected youth leaders, knows a young woman named Annie who became pregnant out of wedlock. A couple of friends told her to abort the baby, but her mom and dad urged her to have the child and allow it to be placed for adoption.

It was a tough assignment—even terrible —but Annie followed through on her parents' counsel. And when all was said and done, she knew that she'd made the right decision. "Yes, I'm okay," she told Joe over the phone through tears of joy. "If you could have seen the look of wonder on that precious mom and dad's faces when I gave them the baby, you never would have needed to worry. That look of appreciation will comfort me forever."[2]

Tears of joy. They'll probably be shed by any young mom who finds the courage to give up her baby for adoption. Chances are she'll be making the best choice for everyone involved. But that's not to say it won't hurt. As Sarah, Adrienne, and Leslie all have recognized, it's extremely difficult to carry a child for nine months, go through labor and childbirth, and then hand your infant son or daughter over to someone else.

The sum of the matter is this: There is no such thing as an "easy" way out of an unplanned, out-of-wedlock pregnancy. How much better to save sex for marriage, where the safety net of the family is there to catch the child and nurture those natural ties!

Sexually Transmitted Diseases: A Modern Epidemic

> *I've heard about the lifelong*
> *consequences of STDs. Maybe*
> *my mistake is that I take that*

*with a grain of salt... Maybe I
should pay attention to it a little
bit more.*

—Julie (17)

Medically speaking, it's probably never been riskier to engage in extramarital sex than it is today. Next to colds and the flu, the most common ailments of our time are—you guessed it—sexually transmitted diseases. In fact, the situation can now be accurately described as an epidemic.

Just how widespread is this epidemic? In the United States alone, 15 million people are infected with STDs every year—25 percent of those STDs are among teens.[3] It is estimated that two out of three people who acquire STDs are younger than 25 years of age.[4] And those numbers increase every year. According to the U.S. Department of Health and Human Services, 86 percent of all STD cases affect young people ages 15 through 29![5] No wonder family physician Dr. Richard Barr tells parents that their teenage sons and daughters are growing up in a dangerous world—a world a far more dangerous than the one they knew as kids.

Explosive growth marks the spread of STDs over the past 30 or 40 years. Consider this brief history. Prior to 1960, syphilis and gonorrhea were the only STDs that occurred with any significant frequency in the United States. That's just about the time that "free love" and "sexual liberation" hit the scene. In the 1970s there was an increase in the number and types of STDs, such as chlamydia. In 1976, penicillin-resistant strains of gonorrhea began to surface. In 1981, acquired immune deficiency syndrome (AIDS) was identified and later found to be caused by the human immunodeficiency virus (HIV). By 1982 genital herpes had become common (over 30 million are now infected), and by 1985 the human papillomavirus (HPV) was widespread as well. During the two years prior to 1988, reported cases of congenital syphilis increased four times over. By 1992 one million women, including 200,000 teenagers, suffered from pelvic inflammatory disease (PID), a complication of chlamydia and gonorrhea.[6]

It's a scary picture. And the details aren't pretty.

"I remember early in my career treating a young woman who was in the hospital for a week with temperatures of 103 degrees as a result of PID," says Dr. Joe McIlhaney, an obstetrician/gynecologist who has "seen it all" during his more than 20 years of medical practice. "It led to a ruptured tube and an ovarian abscess. In the end I had to do a hysterectomy on this young lady. She'll be sterile for the rest of her life."

As far as STDs are concerned, anybody who has sexual intercourse with someone outside of marriage is also having sex with all of his or her partner's past sexual partners. In other words, a girl or guy who is planning to have sex with someone who has had sex with multiple partners in the past can probably count on getting an STD from that person.

Not many options there.

Just the Facts ...

> *You don't know whether anyone has an STD. You don't know if people are telling you the truth.*
> —Betsy (15)

> *My friends and I need to know that there are a lot more STDs out there besides AIDS, because that's what's talked about the most.*
>
> —Julie (17)

What exactly are we looking at regarding sexually transmitted diseases? What are the

symptoms, the signs, the long-term consequences? And what about condoms? Do
they *really* protect anybody from the danger
of contracting an STD? Here's a brief run-
down of the facts about the most common
STDs (note: the CDC [Centers for Disease
Control] has now identified more than 30
organisms and syndromes that are recognized as being sexually transmitted).[7]

BACTERIAL INFECTIONS. Syphilis,
gonorrhea, and chlamydia are caused by bac-
teria. That means that they can be treated—at
least in terms of their obvious, immediate
symptoms—with antibiotics like penicillin.
But they can also lead to serious complications, especially if left untreated; and we're
now seeing strains of these organisms that
resist antibiotic treatment.

Syphilis begins with a simple ulcer or
open sore (called a *chancre*) in the genital area.
The lesion goes away by itself within two to
six weeks. But if left untreated, it will be followed within six months by a mild rash and
other changes in the body. A third stage of the
disease may develop years later, involving
life-threatening heart disease, brain and neu-
rological damage, even insanity.

Gonorrhea usually produces dramatic
symptoms in males: a thick discharge from

the penis and painful urination. In women, it's sometimes harder to detect—there may be a mild discharge or pelvic pain—but in some cases it can lead to scarring of the fallopian tubes ... and lifelong infertility.

Chlamydia, now the most common bacterial STD in the United States, may be accompanied by symptoms similar to but milder than those produced by gonorrhea, or no symptoms at all. But in females, chlamydia can lead to PID (pelvic inflammatory disease) and other infections in the uterus and the fallopian tubes, damage to the lining of those tubes, and sterility. Males often can carry the disease without knowing it.

VIRAL INFECTIONS. Diseases like genital herpes, HPV (human papillomavirus), Hepatitis B, HIV (human immunodeficiency virus) and its consequence, AIDS (acquired immune deficiency syndrome), are caused by viruses. This means they cannot be treated with antibiotics. In other words, they are, generally speaking, incurable.

Herpes simplex virus (HSV) is passed by sexual contact. It appears in the form of a cluster of irritating, sometimes painful blisters in the genital area. Once you have it, you have it for life—the blisters can recur repeatedly. If a woman gives birth during one of these outbreaks, the virus may be passed to her baby, and the results can be disastrous—blindness, mental retardation, even death.

Human papillomavirus (HPV) is now one of the most common STDs in the United States[8] —one recent study showed that over 40 percent of college females who are sexually active become infected with it.[9] You can have it without knowing it. Sometimes it causes soft, wartlike growths to appear in the genital area. Sometimes there are no visible symptoms. But the scariest thing about HPV is that it's been proven to cause cancer—cancer of the cervix, the vulva, and the vagina in females, and cancer of the penis in males. How serious is HPV? Let's allow one of its victims—a college graduate now in her 20s—to describe her experience in her own words:

> While I fully acknowledge my grave error and sin and suffer for it daily, I feel someone must warn the teenagers, the single young adults, and anyone else contemplating a sexual encounter that they will later regret it. The government and the media have thoroughly communicated about AIDS; that is not what

this letter is about. I'm writing about my concern over what human papillomavirus can do. It can give cervical dysplasia, leading to cancer of the cervix in teenagers. Certainly this is tragic. But it has many other effects that I have not read anything about. I have had the best physicians available, and they have given up on me. There is no cure and no way out.

At twenty-five, I have remained single and childless. That singleness is imposed upon me by my physical condition. The last four years of my life have been lived with chronic pain, two outpatient surgeries, multiple office biopsies, thousands of dollars in prescriptions, and no hope. The effect of this problem is one of severe, relentless infection. This condition can be so severe that the pain is almost unbearable, and a sexual relationship (or the possibility of marriage) is out of the question. The isolation is like a knife that cuts my heart out daily. Depression, rage, hopelessness, and a drastically affected social and religious life are the result. While I may not be one of the success stories, I am managing to survive, and it is my hope and prayer that someone will make HPV as well known as AIDS. It took me months to get a diagnosis ... Attempts at a cure are not undertaken in a comprehensive way by the medical profession. My confidence is pretty well shattered. Physicians say they are seeing HPV more commonly. Females are being sentenced to a life of watching others live, marry, and have babies—none of which they can do themselves. [10]

Hepatitis B is a viral infection of the liver. The symptoms are flulike—fever, nausea, and jaundice—and in most cases the disease goes away after running its course. But about 5 percent of the people who contract it become chronic carriers. Chronic infections can lead to cirrhosis (scarring) or even cancer of the liver. And active infections can be passed from mother to child in pregnancy.

HIV and *AIDS* are, of course, the sexually transmitted diseases that get the most airplay these days. This virus is transmitted through semen, vaginal secretions, blood, and breast milk. It's no longer limited to homosexuals, intravenous drug users, and others with high-risk lifestyles. You *are* in greater danger of contracting it if you have many sexual partners, but a single sexual encounter is all it takes. After causing flulike symptoms, the virus can remain in your body for many years without giving any signs of its presence. Eventually it destroys the immune system, leaving its victim vulnerable to all kinds of infections and some forms of cancer.

Trust a Condom?

So what about condoms? Will they keep you safe if you choose to have sex with someone who happens to have one of these diseases? What if you *knew* that your partner had AIDS? Would *you* be willing to trust your life to a thin piece of rubber? It's worth thinking about.

Consider this. According to studies, condoms fail to prevent pregnancy 15.8 percent of the time in the first year of use.[11, 12] This is a standardized failure rate—calculated to show a number that applies to all condom users, not just specific demographic groups. Group-specific rates show much higher numbers: among young, unmarried, minority women the rate is 36.3 percent; and among unmarried Hispanic women it is as high as 44.5 percent.[13]

Dr. Richard Barr will testify that condoms

sometimes fail as a contraceptive device: "I personally can vouch for the ineffectiveness of condoms. There I was, married, with four kids, happy that my family was complete— and then along came twins to prove that condoms fail even for those who know a little about contraception!" Lucky for Dr. Barr that, in his case, the failure occurred within the context of marriage and family. His "safety net" enabled him and his wife to welcome their two little "mistakes" with joy!

Now bear in mind that a woman can become pregnant only a few days out of every month. A disease, on the other hand, can be contracted 365 days a year. That raises the stakes considerably!

Stephanie's Story

Stephanie, an attractive, 22-year-old college student, had been convinced condoms were the answer. She made sure her boyfriends were always considerate enough to use one. And they did.

Then one day Stephanie noticed a small growth on her genitals. A biopsy showed this to be a sexually transmitted precancerous lesion. In other words, if Stephanie hadn't noticed this growth or done anything about it, surgery would have been the only option.

Stephanie was beside herself. How could

such a thing have happened to her? Her partners had used a condom *every* time.

Stephanie's experience notwithstanding, the media, the government, and the school systems have invested a lot of time, energy, and money trying to sell us on the idea that condoms will protect sexually active teens from the viral and bacterial infections described above. Is there any truth to that message? It all depends on how you define "protection."

"Condoms will reduce the risk of picking up some STDs," comments Dr. Barr. "Unfortunately, they won't remove the risk completely. Condoms will give absolutely no protection from some STDs. This is partly because condoms may offer less protection because areas of skin not covered by the condom may be infectious or vulnerable to infection."[14] So even if the device functions as intended and no mistakes are made during intercourse, disease can still be transmitted.

Condoms offer some protection from gonorrhea, but for diseases like syphilis and herpes, where the lesions are outside the area of the condom, there is often less protection.

What about human papillomavirus? Unfortunately, condoms do little or nothing to stop the transmission of HPV, because HPV is a disease that covers the entire genital area.[15] And when it comes to AIDS, the studies in which one partner was infected with HIV and the other was not suggest that consistent condom use significantly reduces —but does not eliminate—the risk of transmission of HIV.[16,17] (It should be noted that AIDS is nearly always fatal.)

Add to this the fact that most teens who intend to use condoms never actually follow through; or that condoms, to be effective, must be used both "consistently and correctly." What does that mean? The CDC spells it out with the following checklist:

1. Use a condom with each act of intercourse.
2. Use the condom from start to finish.
3. Use a new condom for each act of intercourse.
4. Put the condom on as soon as the erection occurs and before any sexual contact.
5. Hold the tip of the condom and unroll, leaving empty space at the end of the condom, yet ensuring that no air is trapped in the condom's tip.
6. Adequate lubrication is important, but use only water-based lubricants ... Oil-based lubricants can weaken the condom.

7. Withdraw from the partner immediately after ejaculation, holding
the condom firmly to keep it from
slipping off.[18]

How many young lovers do you think
have any inclination to follow *that* detailed
list of instructions in the middle of a hot and
heavy situation?

Trust a condom? "A foolish gamble!"
says Dr. Dobson. It's hard to argue with that!

Emotional and Relational Risks

*I think it's a risk to have sex
before marriage. I think it can
emotionally scar you.*
—Molly (15)

Diseases—as terrifying and devastating as
they can be—aren't the only risks you run
when you allow yourself to become sexually
involved outside of marriage. Not by a long
shot.

Sex, as we tried to say earlier in this chapter, goes so much deeper than the physical. No
one can ever take a picture of *true* sex. That's
what makes pornography so ridiculously sick,
hollow, and dehumanizing. The *act* of sex is
just the tip of the iceberg. It's the outward

expression of a profound inner reality—a *whole-self connection* with another person in an exclusive, permanent relationship. You can't enter into that kind of connection without becoming involved at every level of your being: physical, psychological, mental, emotional, and spiritual. This is definitely *not* a game.

"Sex is a multidimensional experience, and it has multidimensional consequences," observes Michelle Baranek. "When we have sex with someone, we engage on the most intimate level, and those consequences are not just physical but emotional."

Try this experiment at home (go ahead—it's safe!). Take two sheets of different-colored paper and glue them together. After the glue has had plenty of time to dry, try to pull the two pieces of paper apart. What happens? They separate cleanly, right? *Wrong!* Instead, what you get is rips and tears and shreds, bits of each page clinging to the other. Those two sheets of paper will never be the same as they were before the gluing.

That's how it is with sex. When you share yourself intimately with another person in sexual intercourse, you give away a piece of your heart, a piece of your soul, *that you can never get back again.* A part of you remains connected to that other person—for better or for worse. For as long as life remains. Funny, isn't it, how they never mention that sort of thing in Sex Ed.

What this means is that when your relationship with that "significant other" comes to an end, you're going to experience a lot of pain and heartache. It's not like simply "breaking up" with a steady boyfriend or girlfriend. It's more profound than that. The ripping and tearing of those deep, mystical bonds can be excruciating. Says Dr. Hager, "One result of sexual activity is a great deal of ambivalence in the emotional feelings of the teens involved. On the one hand, they want to believe that they have bonded to an individual, that they have interrelated with that individual in a permanent way. But the truth of the matter is that most of those relationships end."

And guess what? In many instances, premature sex is actually the *cause* of the breakup. "Having sex ruins a relationship," says 16-year-old Brent, who knows from experience. "I lost respect for myself and my partner."

Alicia, another one of Joe White's many friends, can tell a similar story. She related it to Joe in a letter:

I had a friend named Rick. Rick and I would talk forever. We became so close that our feelings developed into more romance than just friendship.... Then one night it happened— we had sex. It was worse than I could even imagine ...

Rick walked me to my car and asked me what was wrong. I burst into tears. I told him that I hated it. I never wanted to do it again. Then Rick told me that he loved me, and the weirdest thing was that I couldn't tell him that I loved him back.

In the long run, experiences like Alicia's can contribute to the development of a very painful and unhealthy lifelong pattern: a pattern of relating to the opposite sex in a series of easy-come, easy-go so-called "permanent connections."

Bond. *Break.* Bond. *Break.* Bond. *Break.*

The frightening thing is, it becomes a pattern that's very difficult to change—even after you find someone with whom you really want to settle down in marriage.

No wonder estimates of the divorce rate among adults who were sexually active in their teens run extremely high. Dr. Hager puts the figure at 75 to 80 percent, an assertion that dovetails with findings of sociologists at the Universities of Chicago and

Michigan, who report that "Those who cohabit [live together] before marriage have substantially higher divorce rates than those who do not; the recorded differentials range from 50 to 100 percent."[19]

It doesn't take a genius to see that the biggest risk of premarital sex is the heart-risk. And heartache can be one of the most difficult diseases of all to cure.

Weighing the Risks

> *I think a lot of people know about STDs. They're just not thinking realistically about it...like, "Oh, I can't get it."*
> —Susan (18)

> *A lot of teenagers think that STDs are so far away, and it's kind of an unrealistic issue. But yet it's really close and it's so dangerous, but you just feel invincible when you're a teenager.*
> —Mark (15)

Given the dangers, why do so many teens choose to become involved in premarital sexual activity? Are they ignorant of the risks? Do they need more facts? Dr. Hager doesn't think so. "They have the head knowledge," he says. "Very often they don't have the heart knowledge."

It all goes back to the something we talked about in Chapter 4: The Illusion of the "Invincible I." The idea that "it won't happen to me."

As Dr. Hager says, "What we have to recognize is that teenagers are risk-takers. We are all risk-takers when we're young. We're willing to take a risk and ignore the long-term consequences. That's why you can't isolate teenage sexual activity by itself. It's not in a vacuum. It belongs in a box with other risk-taking behaviors, like the use of cigarettes, alcohol, and drugs; risk-taking behaviors like carrying weapons or belonging to groups or gangs that engage in violence. All of that's in the box connected to sexual activity."

To a certain extent, risk-taking is legitimate. Risk is an important part of the adventure of living. But—and this is the crucial point—it's foolish to take *unnecessary* risks. A legitimate risk matches the value of the thing you hope to gain by taking it. It would be stupid, for instance, to go charging into the ocean at riptide...unless your five-year-old son is caught in the undertow. Similarly, it's insane to expose yourself to the perils—

physical, medical, emotional, and spiritual—
of a sexual relationship unless you're prepared to go the distance, give up your own
selfish desires, and lay down your life for
your partner—*whatever* means that may take.

◎　◎　◎

Nate and Jeff were startled out of their quiet
disagreement by a sudden presence of third
person at the table. It was Kim, who blew in
like a whirlwind, sat down uninvited, and
immediately let loose with a fast and furious
gale of words.

"Can you believe it?" she hissed, looking
over her shoulder. "She's the third person in
our class this year!"

"What are you talking about?" asked
Nate. "Who's the third person to what?"

"Lisa," answered Kim in a confidential
tone. "I just heard that she tested positive. I
wonder who she got it from."

Jeff lifted his eyes from the note he'd been
scribbling in the margin of his philosophy
textbook—*risk: proportionate to value*—and
gave Nate a pointed look.

"Yeah," he said. "And I wonder who she
gave it to."

Nate wiped his mouth with the back of
his hand.

6

Choices

Two soldiers, comrades-in-arms, came tramping along a road together, making their way home from the Spartan battlefront ... helmets dusty and dull ... tunics soiled and torn ... shields dented ... spear points blunted ... sandals worn through ... faces and limbs riddled with scars.

Around a bend and over a small hill the road suddenly forked.

"Which path are we to choose?" said the first soldier, a gaunt man with a sharp chin and sandy hair and whiskers.

"I do not know," said his comrade, a stocky, swarthy, sinewy fighter.

"*I* do," said a voice close at hand. They

turned to see an old graybeard, leaning on a twisted staff beneath a dark outcropping of rock at the side of the road.

"You?" said the first soldier. "And just who are you?"

"A resident of the neighborhood," he answered. "One who knows the way better than you do—through long experience."

"And how do we know you're to be trusted?" asked the second soldier, eyeing the old man narrowly.

"You don't," said the traveler briefly, "although this may serve to sway your opinion." With that he held out his right hand. On his index finger he wore a large gold ring bearing the seal of the Athenian Assembly.

"How fortunate!" exclaimed the first soldier. "As it happens, we are on our way home—to Athens. Can you tell us which fork of the road will take us there?"

"I can tell you this much," answered the greybeard. "To the left the road follows a rippling stream over gentle slopes through a green and fruitful valley. It's an easy walk. But just beyond the first great bend in the brook, *that* road takes a sweeping turn to the south and heads straight into Sparta itself. If you go that way you will be heading straight into the arms of your enemies. I hardly need point out the dangers associated with such a course of action.

"The other fork—the one to the right," continued their counselor, "will seem to you a poor choice in the beginning, for it is narrow, rocky, overgrown here and there with thistles and thorns, and often hard to discern. But you must take my word for it: That way lies your road home."

"Well, Cleanthes," said the sandy-bearded soldier to his companion when the old man had finished, "it seems our path is clear. To the right, then?" He turned an inquiring glance toward his friend....

◎　◎　◎

I think we know enough about sex. I mean, you have to know the basic stuff. After that, it's your own thing. It's your own responsibility. So you think about it and you decide what to do.

　　　　　　　　—Leah

Life is choices, because America is free and you can do whatever you want.

　　　　　　　　—Allison

None of us can live without knowledge. Accurate information does more than inform—it *empowers*. To know is to rise to a new level of personal capability—and responsibility. But just to know isn't enough.

If you've read this far, it's just possible (at least we hope so!) that you *know* more than you did when you first opened the book. Stored away in the archives of your brain is a file of information that wasn't there before. Maybe you've even been thinking seriously about that information and with it have formed—or strengthened—some opinions of your own about sexual activity outside of marriage. If so, you're on the right track. You're exactly where you should be. But it doesn't mean a thing unless you have the courage to go a step further. All the information and knowledge in the world won't do anybody an ounce of good unless it is turned into the raw material for something even more important: choices, decisions … and *action*.

I can't help but think of the news story of the young woman driving through the night and the rain who came to a set of barricades in the road with a sign that said "BRIDGE OUT." Investigators found evidence that she carefully maneuvered her minivan around the barricades and drove straight off an embankment into a black and raging river.

She had the information. She simply

chose not to believe it or apply it. What the sign said, she reasoned, couldn't be what it meant. That would be much too inconvenient. So she didn't turn around. And that was the last decision she would ever make.

The Education Deception

> *Self-control is an important factor. I mean, you're ultimately making the decision. A lot of people get into trouble because of passion and stuff. It happens impromptu. But along with self-control, it's how much you're thinking about your future.*
> —Jeremy

There's a myth at large in the world today. It's the idea that Education (with a capital "E") can and will solve all our problems. Education is power—power to change the world. Teach people the right things, and they'll automatically *do* the right things.

Or so the story goes.

What better way to fix the twin problems of teenage pregnancy and epidemic rates of sexually transmitted diseases? Accurate information is all that's lacking. So fund the programs with more tax dollars, give kids the facts and figures, and they'll be sensible enough to draw the right conclusions. End of discussion.

But there are a couple of difficulties with this theory. First, when it comes to sex education, there are both good and bad varieties on the market. And although the good has been gaining ground, the bad has dominated the market for the past couple of decades or so (we touched on this point back in Chapter 2). On the whole, the "safe sex" message that says teens can't control their sexual urges and had better learn how to "protect" themselves instead has served as the centerpiece of the sex education curricula used in the public schools.

As the years roll by, we're finding out that this approach doesn't really help anybody make wiser decisions about sex. As a matter of fact, it seems to have aggravated the problem. After two decades of well-intentioned sex education and contraceptive distribution programs in the schools, the House Select Committee on Children, Youth, and Families concluded that "there has been no change in the percentage of sexually active teens who become pregnant, but there has been a huge increase in the percentage of teens who are sexually active. And this increase in sexual activity has led to a proportionate increase in pregnancies to unmarried teens."[1]

According to researcher Dinah Richard, nearly $2 billion was spent on federally funded family planning programs between 1971 and 1981 in an attempt to reduce unwanted pregnancies. Strangely, during those 10 years teen pregnancy rates climbed 48.3 percent and teen abortions skyrocketed 133 percent.[2] So in this case, information—wrong-headed information—has only made a bad situation worse.

But there's another big flaw in the theory that knowledge can save us, and it has to do with human nature. It's a question of will: of stubbornness and selfishness and hardened hearts. Like the 10-year-old boy who was swept to his death when he climbed a fence to play in a rain-swollen creek, we all do things that we *know* aren't smart or good for us. Why? Because we *want* to. Even good and helpful information about sex—the kind of information this book is meant to provide—accomplishes nothing if it isn't applied and translated into action. It's the "want to" factor that has to change if our headful of knowledge is to do us any good.

"That Does Not Compute"

Q: *Are you going to wait until you're married to have sex?*

Courtney: *I'm not going to wait. I don't think so.*
Q: *Why? Do you know the risks involved?*
Courtney: *Yeah.*

Will: *Abstinence is the only way you can actually be sure that you won't get someone pregnant or get an STD.*
Q: *What about you? Are you going to do it?*
Will: *Have sex before I'm married? Probably.*

Listen to enough junior high and high school students talk about their sexual attitudes and activities and you'll begin to pick up on something pretty strange and scary: knowledge and information make surprisingly little difference. Most of us have an amazing capacity to act in ways that run contrary to everything we know and believe. That's particularly true with a force as powerful as the sexual drive. If the facts don't fit in with what you're feeling, just file them someplace else. Then go ahead and follow your impulses. Pull around those barricades on the road and hope the bridge will be there anyway.

Sarah is a good example. Remember,

Sarah is a Christian, active in her church youth group, and claimed to believe that sex outside of marriage is wrong. But somehow that didn't stop her from becoming sexually involved with her boyfriend. She and Jimmy had heard as much about condoms, STDs, and "safe sex" as any other kids in school. Yet Sarah not only chose to have sex with Jimmy, she chose to do it without protection.

Heather Jamison, today a happily married mother of three, had a similar experience. She and her boyfriend Brian were the ideal teen Christian couple. He was a member of the National Honor Society, an all-district athlete, former president of the youth group, and teacher-chosen peer counselor; she was a deacon's daughter, a cheerleader, and model student.

Surprise! Pregnant at 18, Heather rushed into marriage—a difficult and rocky union for the first couple of years—with Brian. Of all people, you'd have thought that *they* would have known better.

"It's amazing how many Christian youths who get pregnant later admit they never used any protection," writes Heather. "Brian and I didn't. At least not consistently. I just assumed cheerleaders and churchgoers didn't get pregnant.... 'Are you just plain dumb?' my sister asked me after I confided in her about my sexual activity. Her words and harsh tone were shocking to me. I'd never considered myself dumb."[3]

Or ask Leah. She, too, is well-versed in the possible consequences of premarital sex. "Some risks about having sex before marriage: You can get pregnant—that's a risk. You can get some disease. There's also a possibility that you will get married and get a disease from your partner. There's not a lot of people you can trust.... You have to be responsible. It's not just like, 'Okay, let's go have sex,' and that's fine. I think it's something serious." She adds, "I do believe in God. I go to church every Sunday."

But strangely enough, for Leah, the bottom line has little or nothing to do with God or consequences or responsibility or facts about pregnancy and STDs. "Should you wait or shouldn't you wait until you get married?" she asks. "I don't think you should if you really love somebody, if you can trust the person with whom you're going to have sex."

Does that compute?

Liz, an intelligent young lady who talks openly about her attitudes toward sex, says, "I think sexual activity before marriage really is a gamble, and I don't think that it's for me." Regarding the benefits of abstinence, she comments, "If I were to wait, I think it would make it more special when I finally do meet that person with whom I'm willing to share this really special thing. And people might look at me in a more respectful light."

Sounds good so far. Liz, however, has left herself a back door...just in chase she changes her mind. "If I meet someone I really trust, and if I am incredibly safe about it, it's okay to have sex before marriage." (It's a funny thing how one little escape clause can change the whole nature of a commitment.)

Then there's Matt, who claims that "Abstinence is the only 100 percent sure way not to get pregnant or catch an STD," and who figures that he'll wait a while to have sex—probably until about age 16.

And Maggie—who clearly understands the purpose of school-based Sex Ed and the dangers of premarital intimacy: "I think some of the consequences of having sex are getting pregnant and catching diseases.... That's why they educate us in school. That's why we have health classes and things like 'Peer Group,' that help us understand the consequences and the dangers of sex at a young age." A good explanation—but apparently it doesn't have much to do with her *personal* decisions about sex: "Will I have sex before I get married? I don't know. I think it depends...on the way I feel about it."

The conclusion is hard to escape: It's not what you know, but what you *do* with what you know that counts. And different people do amazingly different things with the same information.

Two Roads

Everyone makes choices, whether they think they do or not. Refuse to choose, and— guess what? You've just chosen! It's possible to ignore the facts and figures, to put them on the back burner for a while. But that doesn't mean anyone gets a vacation from the business of life. We *have* to keep moving ahead along one path or another. And our choices— even if they're non-choices—have a profound effect on where we end up.

Let's consider two teens who chose two different roads. Two different ways of handling knowledge and responding to truth. As it turns out, Jack and Allison are a study in contrasts.

Jack

Jack has discovered some of the harsher realities of premarital sex the hard way— through personal experience. He can speak clearly and articulately about the pain and hurt that follow when sexual activity takes place outside of its rightful context. He knows what the ideal sexual relationship *should* look like. And when he talks on this subject, there's a tone of authority in his voice that takes you by surprise. You have a feeling that he's been there.

It all started when he was only six years old. That's when Jack became another victim of child sexual molestation. It's a tragically common story: "I did only what I was told," he says, "because when you're that age, that's what you think." It happened again when he was 11.

In time, the negative effects of his experience began to surface. "I was very lost, very confused. I found out how women get raped. It was like reversed roles. You very rarely hear of men getting raped. Well, I would say, in a way, I was that man, or I was that woman, being sexually abused or invaded. I know how it feels to be invaded. So I believe sex should be mutual. It should be out of respect. It should not be a game. It should not be something that you just want to do."

At 15 he found himself falling into a familiar pattern. Once again the reversed-role syndrome raised its ugly head, only this time the invader was not an abusive adult— it was a girlfriend, a sexually active peer who had ideas of her own about the course their relationship was going to take. For reasons he can hardly explain, Jack bent to her will.

"I was actually pushed into having intercourse for the first time...and I wasn't using protection, either. I was asked not to use it on her request. I was very, very scared."

Guilt? Jack says no—that's not his style. Regrets? Yes; at the time, "I kind of regretted it. I wished I hadn't done that." How about long-term debts to pay? No mistake about that: "I don't think a lot of teens know about the emotional side of sex until they experience it. I didn't know about it until I lost my virginity, and it was devastating. I wasn't ready, and it really had an impact on me."

Jack's emotional wounds have made him almost amazingly sensitive. Out of his experience come some incredibly perceptive statements about the meaning of human sexuality. His definition of love, for instance, reads like a perfect description of the marriage relationship: "Love is when you pull all the options together, all the consequences, and make them one thing before you choose to do something that could affect the rest of your life. Love is when you're sharing mutual respect, and you're actually becoming one person, one body, one mind, and you're really consummating a relationship."

Listen to Jack long enough and you'll get

the impression that he also has some appreciation for the priceless value of virginity. At least his words reflect some degree of *knowledge* about the subject. "I feel that virginity is very important," he says, "because it is part of somebody's *spiritual person*. Once that's taken, you can never get it back."

He's keenly aware, too, of the dangers of mixing drugs and alcohol with relationships between the sexes, and he's far from ignorant when it comes to the threat of STDs—"The best source of information about STDs would be people who have it. I know people who have it."

And Jack is under no illusions about the relative "safety" of "safe sex": "Having sex with protection is less risky than having it without protection. But there's really no way—that I find—to judge how risky it really is. There will always be a risk as long as you are having intercourse or any type of sex."

Based on his experience, what's Jack's recommendation to his peers? "I totally agree that abstinence is the safest way, the most effective way to be 'pure.' You know, not getting pregnant, not getting STDs. That is true.

"I didn't really give my virginity away willingly," he continues. "It was kind of taken from me. I didn't know who I was. But now that I have more confidence, I am willing and able to say no. I'm willing to help other people who can't say no. I know the information. I know how it feels, and I have a strong ability to empathize because I have been invaded.

"Abstinence is strength," he concludes. "If you can abstain, that shows a strength because you have that will, that power, that self-confidence. It's that fight, that drive, that makes you a stronger person because you have an inner strength that most people won't have."

All of this would lead the average reader to conclude that Jack is personally and unswervingly committed to abstinence; that he's saving himself for marriage; that he follows his own advice and demonstrates his self-confidence by saying no.

Unfortunately, that's not the case. "Personally, I *am* currently having intercourse," he admits when asked point-blank about it. "I feel that if you know the information, then you can protect yourself."

Apparently it's pretty easy to do the exact opposite of what you know to be best for yourself. Jack is a case in point.

Allison

Allison has a different way of handling the "information." Just 13 years old, she has sharply defined opinions on the subject of sex outside of marriage, and has chosen deliberately to put those opinions to work in her life.

"Some of today's teens," muses Allison, "are wild and fun, and some of them are carefree. I think they may end up somewhere they don't want to be. Others are smart and fun, too. You can have fun and still be smart." Allison is pretty smart herself.

How smart? Well, like Jack, she knows all about the risks and dangers of sexual activity outside of marriage. Unlike Jack, she hasn't gained her information from personal experience. Instead, she's been wise enough to listen to people who are older and wiser than she is. People like her parents.

"My parents told me about sex around the time when I was in third grade—so I basically knew about it before it was explained to me in school.

"They told me about the consequences and explained to me what might happen. I knew right off the bat that I wasn't going to get involved in that kind of stuff."

What consequences? That's easy, says Allison: "I could get pregnant. I could get a sexually transmitted disease. I could get into lots of trouble in other areas, like drinking and stuff—or even committing suicide because of depression."

Allison knows better than to trust a condom. "It's just a skinny piece of rubber," she
says. "They have holes in them—little air
holes—and the holes are too big to protect
you against STDs."

She's also pretty savvy when it comes to
getting inside the mind of the opposite sex:
"Some boyfriends can get you involved in
sex. If I were to go to school and just pick the
cutest guy there, he'd probably have taken
advantage of some of the other girls. He
doesn't really want a girlfriend...he's just
looking for looks and sex."

And her thoughts on the meaning and
value of her own virginity go straight to the
heart of the matter. "The gift of virginity is
very important to me. I can save myself for
my husband, and if he saves himself for me,
then that's our present to each other and we
don't have to share it with anybody.

"I've heard that it's okay to have sex. I
don't believe that's true. I could become like
that in 10 minutes, but *they* can never
become a virgin again. I'm proud to be a virgin, and I know that I'm saving myself for
my husband."

Perceptive observations on a complex
side of life from an inexperienced 13-year-
old. But Allison hasn't left these thoughts in
the category of "interesting ideas." She's

turned them into something unbelievably powerful—the basis of a personal commitment. "It's my decision if I want to have sex or not. It's not my teacher's, it's not my friend's, it's *my* decision. And I have vowed not to have sex before I get married."

Allison has a strong faith in God. But she doesn't stop there. She has thought carefully about how that faith relates to her everyday life. She puts her faith to work. It's the crucial factor in every decision she makes. And that includes decisions about sex.

"God plays the biggest role in my life," she says. "He's my best friend. When nobody else is there, He's there, and He helps me make all my decisions. I have to make sure that He is number one in my life, and He'll help me all the way."

She's not shy about it. Allison has made her choice. And it's a choice she can live with.

Do the *Right* Thing

To know is not enough.

It is never enough.

You have to *do* something with what you know. That might have been the end of the story except for one troublesome detail: It's possible to do the *wrong* thing.

Jack and Allison are both well acquainted with the facts about condoms, pregnancy,

STDs, and the emotional consequences of premarital sex. Both of them have made personal choices about sexual activity based on the same information. But their choices are as different as night and day. One says "I won't"; the other says "I do and I will—regardless." They can't both be right.

That's the real conclusion of the matter. It's not enough to know and choose—you have to choose *right*. "Choice" is a popular notion today. This is America, after all, and everyone gets to determine his or her own course. Everyone agrees with that. But it's not quite so trendy to insist that some choices are better than others—that some decisions are right and some are wrong. Hard realities like unwanted pregnancy, sexually transmitted diseases, and broken lives just demonstrate that it's possible to be trendy, tolerant … and dangerously off track. As Jack says, "Sex is a matter of life. And nowadays, it's also a matter of death." Not much room for personal preference there.

◎　◎　◎

"…I choose the left fork, Lysander," the second soldier answered firmly. His companion stared at him in disbelief.

"But why? Did you not hear what our friend had to say?"

"As clearly as you heard it yourself."

"And do you have good reason to doubt his truthfulness?"

"None in particular."

"And did you see the ring upon his finger?"

"With my own two eyes."

"Why, then," pleaded Lysander in exasperation, "do you insist on taking a road that, according to everything we've been told, leads directly into danger?"

"Because it is my choice," responded his comrade, "and I choose to do so."

And so they parted ways. Lysander took the path to the right, traveling with his gray-bearded guide, and in two days' time arrived in Athens to the great relief of his family and friends.

Cleanthes took the left fork and was never seen again.

7

Consequences

The big picture is what's going to happen down the line. One night of sex—what are the consequences of that, and how is it going to affect your life forever?

—Julie (17)

"Step right up. Play the game. You pays your money and you takes your chances!"

That's what the hawkers at carnivals used to say. Maybe there was a hidden warning in that invitation: When you take chances, you can never be sure of the outcome. You make your choices and you live with the consequences.

Some people gamble and get away with it—at least for a while. Some take risks and seem to beat the odds. When the game is going your way, it's hard to see any reason to listen to the killjoys, the spoilsports, and the prophets of doom.

But what happens when your luck and your roll of quarters run out at the same time? Or when the statistics turn against you? What do you do when you wake up one morning only to find that theory has become life—*your* life? Sarah, Adrienne, and Leslie have all had an opportunity to think long and hard about the answers to those questions.

Sarah: Stepping Off the Train

"I knew I was having sex," says Sarah, "but I didn't think I could get pregnant."

Oh yes, she could. And did.

Sarah could have said no to Jimmy. If you had asked her at the time, she probably would have told you that saying no was "the right thing to do." But for some deep, complex, and very personal reasons, she decided that saying no just wasn't worth the effort. "I was sexually molested when I was three," she explains, "and I'd been raped twice in ninth grade. By the time I reached my sophomore year I had the idea that saying no didn't work. It seemed useless." So she said yes—and kept on saying it...time after time after time.

That's when she began to experience severe abdominal pains. The doctor, who hypothesized she might be suffering from an ovarian cyst, did an ultrasound to get a better look at what was going on inside her body. He also gave her a pregnancy test.

"An hour later they called me at my house and told me I was pregnant. That's when reality set in, I guess. I was shocked. When I got that phone call, it felt like I had been riding on a train for so long, and all of a sudden the train just stopped and let me off. I had to face up to it. Had to walk on my own—get on my own two feet and move on."

She was 16 years old, unmarried, and pregnant—a Christian who, in theory, didn't believe in abortion or sex outside of marriage. This wasn't part of the plan. She'd been sexually active for several months, yet she was shocked and surprised to hear that she was really and truly pregnant. Nature has a powerful way of succeeding.

As might have been expected, Sarah's parents "freaked out." And another thing happened that Sarah never could have predicted while she was having sex with Jimmy and feeling that this, after all, was what love was supposed to be like. Their relationship began to sour, going from bad to worse.

Jimmy's attitude toward Sarah became increasingly domineering and controlling. He decided that he had the authority to choose her friends for her and tell her where she could and couldn't go. And his violent and abusive tendencies became more than just tendencies. For a while, Sarah put up with it and played along, supposing that, somehow or other, it was *meant* to be this way. "I guess I thought that we were going to get married and live happily ever after—like the fairy tale."

But Jimmy had other ideas. In the course of time, *two* wedding dates were made and canceled—canceled because he felt he "wasn't ready." A series of painful and ugly breakups and make-ups followed. Somehow, no matter how bad things got, Sarah felt that she had to hold on to her baby's father. "We'd break up, and every time, within 12 hours, I would be begging, literally begging, for him to get back together with me."

The crisis came when Jimmy promised to marry Sarah if she'd move in with him six months before the wedding date. Strange as it sounds, that, for her, was the last straw.

"I've compromised my values with you

enough already!" she told him. "I'm not going to do it anymore!"

The greatest miracles and mysteries are often the smallest. Even something as small as a change of heart. Finding the strength of will to take a stand.

Sarah had been sleeping with Jimmy for months. She had conceived his child outside of wedlock. In the name of "love" she had allowed him to run her life. But now, for reasons she didn't fully understand, she suddenly found her voice and discovered the courage to speak for herself. When he pushed her an inch too far, she discovered that she had some moral backbone after all. "I didn't want to get back together with him," she says. "So I prayed. I said, 'God, if this is what You want me to do, give me the strength to do it.' And He did." Sarah had learned to say no. It hadn't been easy. It hadn't been without tears. But somehow, in the days to come, it seemed like the best thing she had ever done.

She gave birth to a healthy baby boy and named him Jimmy after his father. Abortion was never an option. "I know this might sound really dumb—dumb because I'm a Christian and I don't believe in sex before marriage, though I did it anyway—but I definitely do not believe in abortion. I remember thinking, *There is a life inside of me. Whether you can see it or not, whether its heart is beating yet or not, it's still growing inside of me, and I'm not going to put it to death."*

Sarah didn't think it could happen to her, but it did. Sarah had been fooled. Through bad thinking—or not thinking at all—she had tripped herself up and fallen into a deep hole of her own making. At that point she could have dug the hole even deeper by looking for the "easy" way out. But somehow she found the courage and determination to choose the narrow, rocky, upward road.

She said no to Jimmy. And she said yes to the life growing inside her.

It would be nice if we could say that the story—at least the darker side of the story—ends there. But Jimmy wasn't happy with Sarah's decision. He wouldn't take "no" for an answer. One night in January, he showed up with a gun, broke into Sarah's house, raped her, and shot himself in front of their child. Fortunately, the wound wasn't fatal. Jimmy was taken into custody, his illegal status was discovered, and deportation procedures began.

"My life hasn't been anything near ideal," says Sarah. "It's all because of the mistakes I made by having sex before marriage. Everyone wants to have an ideal life, like a fairy tale. But once I put myself in that position, my life became more of a nightmare than a fantasy. Emotionally, I've been in turmoil for the last couple of years. It's been very, very hard. I have to see a counselor now, and that's something I never thought I'd do."

What began behind the counter at Taco Bell continues even today. In a very real way, it will never end. Sarah knows there will be consequences for her baby, too. "On the whole, I'm glad that Jimmy is being deported. But in some ways I'm not. That's my baby's father."

Leslie: The Bride Wore Blue

The cheerleading competition just a bad memory, Leslie sat in a dingy little office talking with the receptionist, awaiting her turn with one of the clinic doctors. Her boyfriend sat outside in the car. She felt lonely, depressed, and intimidated. And things didn't get any better once she was asked to step inside.

After an examination that lasted about two and a half minutes, the man in the lab coat snapped off his gloves, crossed his arms, looked at her coldly, and said, "Okay, you're pregnant. You're in a big mess. *Now* what are you going to do?"

She wasn't sure, but she had an idea. "I was thinking in the back of my mind that maybe I could work this out for myself. Maybe I could get this boy to marry me and the two of us could begin a happy life together on our own with our baby. I didn't even realize what was happening to me."

She walked out of the office, crossed the parking lot with slow steps, and leaned into the car window with a smile. "Guess what?" she said to her boyfriend. "We're going to have a baby!" That's when her scheme hit its first snag.

"His face just dropped," she recalls. "I watched fear overtake him. It overtook me, too. I knew this wasn't anything that I was going to be able to pretend my way through."

She was 16. He was 18. Her mom and dad reacted with anger, and the parents of the prospective groom firmly opposed any wedding. "I told my boyfriend that I wanted to get married and keep the baby. That's what girls did back then. But it didn't go over too well with his parents. They began to tell me horrible stories about him, things I didn't know. They said that if I really knew the truth, I wouldn't want to be with him. But I just covered my ears and refused to listen."

So late that summer a small ceremony took place in her mother's living room— family, a few friends, a hopeful young woman, and an ambivalent young man. The bride wore blue. "I didn't really understand why they wouldn't let me wear white. I knew nothing about the symbolism of the white: purity, virginity. Virginity wasn't talked about in those days. It was expected."

The vows were taken, the prayers said, the pronouncements made. Then the groom disappeared into the kitchen for the rest of the evening. Later, when the last of the guests had gone, the two of them climbed into his Corvair and drove away. "It was strange—to leave and not come home, not even call and let someone know that you're not coming home. But that was just the beginning: my first clue that the security of my old life was passing away. The whole feeling of safety and security was totally snatched away from me that night."

It wasn't long before those prophetic feelings began to find fulfillment. Leslie returned to school in September for her senior year. She was two months pregnant. "Everyone at school already knew. I would sit by myself in the cafeteria, walk to my classes by myself. Nobody would talk to me. I felt completely alone. I was used to having my phone ringing off the wall. Now I was living with a teenage husband and didn't even have a phone.

"I was still a student, and I wanted to participate in Homecoming. School activities like that had always been important to me. I was only two or three months pregnant and wasn't showing very much. But they asked me not to be involved. That hurt. It was completely humiliating."

But that wasn't the worst of it. Life on the home front wasn't turning out as she had expected. "Within the first two weeks of married life my new husband began abusing me incredibly—slapping me around, kicking me in the stomach, staying out all night. He called me horrible names and told me how fat and ugly I was, how no one would want me, not even him, and that he was going to spend the rest of his life making me pay for what I had done to him. He left me alone constantly. I didn't have a car and didn't know how to drive. I was a prisoner in my own home."

That kind of treatment took its toll. Leslie's self-esteem plunged, and she began to think of herself as completely worthless. "I was suicidal. I really didn't want to live anymore. I thought quite often about going up to a bluff near our house and just jumping off. I wanted to end the nightmare. I found myself married to someone who really didn't care about me, who didn't love me, who constantly abused me verbally and physically. I had no family or friends."

Such a short time since she had given herself away so easily! And all for nothing. Her hopes and dreams had all gone down to ruin. The hugs had turned into slaps and kicks. The desperate longing for love went bitterly unmet.

Her son was born in March of that year—over what would have been Spring Break. He was a big baby: nine pounds, eight ounces. "For me, a skinny little high school girl, that was not fun. I had no clue about what happens in a delivery room—it had never even occurred to me what that experience was going to be like."

Labor and delivery traumatized Leslie. No one had done anything to prepare her for the experience. And 25 years ago, social attitudes toward pregnant teenagers were far less congenial than they are today. She remembers being mocked by the nurses and laughed at by the doctors and the anesthesiologist. "They all thought it was very funny to teach a teenage girl a lesson, to make sure she never got in this mess again. It was horrific."

A new mother at 17, trapped in an abusive and loveless marriage, Leslie looked around and found herself in a world she had never imagined on the night she lied to her mother and slipped off with her boyfriend to a dark, secluded spot. "As a teenage mom, my life changed from this happy-go-lucky, high-school-good-time affair, to what I call trauma and terror. It was just crisis after crisis. I found myself asking, *How did I get here? Who wrote me into this script? I'm not this girl.*

"The stigma of teen pregnancy was always with me. In a way, it's still with me today. People always reacted to me like, 'Oh, you must have been one of those girls who, uh, slept around and came from the bad side of town and had no goals and really gave herself away easily.' And I always felt like, 'No! I was a girl who was going to college, who was having a great time in high school, but who found someone by mistake and ended up in a place I never wanted to go.'

"I was someone who always laughed, who loved life and had a capacity to soak everything in. This boy took my laughter and didn't even give me tears in exchange, because he left me in a condition where I couldn't even cry anymore. He left me with a blank, plain heart.

"You know," she concludes, "in retrospect it strikes me that there was one sense in which my fears were valid. If I had not had sex with this boy, he would have left me in a heartbeat. He would have been on to something else and I would have been on to something else. Back then, it just seemed so final, like my life was going to be over if I said no. But actually, my life would have gone on. And I would have avoided a decade of anguish and pain."

Adrienne: A Bear Named Gracie

"Sex is fun while you're doing it," says Adrienne. "But the consequences—well, let's just say I had no idea that the decisions I was making would have the lifelong effects they did."

Not that she made that discovery immediately. In Adrienne's case, the lesson took a little longer to become clear. She wasn't one of those girls who wakes up the morning after, feeling dirty and used and remorseful. On the whole, the party her friends threw for her the night after her 16th birthday suited her mood exactly. She was perfectly happy to join them in celebrating her initiation into the Fellowship of Former Virgins.

But changes were coming.

Seven months, one abortion, and one boyfriend later, Adrienne and Clint (her new lover) were driving north, headed for a clinic in another town where they could terminate her *second* pregnancy (she had conceived while on Depo-Provera, a so-called "fail-safe" contraceptive injection) without drawing too much attention to themselves or running into anyone who might happen to know them. It was going to be an expensive procedure: Money was a problem, and she had let things go a little longer this time—five months to be exact.

"I didn't tell anybody for five months. I carried that baby and that secret around with me every day for five months, because I didn't feel like there was anybody in my life I could talk to about that. And the only reason I eventually did decide to tell the baby's father was that I needed money for an abortion. It would have been a very late-term abortion, a very costly abortion, which is why I finally went to the baby's father. I needed $2,500."

The *first* abortion had been costly enough—if not in dollars and cents, then in unexpected emotional liabilities. Although Adrienne knew that the blob of cells growing inside her was actually a child, a person, a living human being—she knew enough about biology to have figured that out—what she didn't know until after the abortion was that she would have such strong feelings for that child.

"I remember going home the night of my abortion and just crying myself to sleep. It was a very painful night. I was very upset. I remember just holding my stomach, wishing I could have that child back."

And now she and Clint were speeding down the road toward a *second* abortion.

Clint's finances, however, weren't any better off than hers. He didn't have $2,500 on hand—or anything close. That's why, before pulling onto the highway, they stopped off at the home of a married couple he knew. "We talked some friends of his into giving us their credit card. We were going to put the abortion on their card and then pay them back."

And so, borrowed plastic in hand, Clint and Adrienne drove into the clinic parking lot. "When we got there," she says, "I had an ultrasound done. They determined that I was 25 and a half weeks pregnant and told me that I had to start the procedure that afternoon or they wouldn't do it. I guess I was that close to their limit for late-term abortions."

After the nurses finished the paperwork and administered some preliminary tests, they were preparing to take Adrienne downstairs to the procedure room when the clinic decided she had better settle financial arrangements before going any further. Dressed in jeans and a hospital gown and armed with the credit card, Adrienne approached the receptionist's desk, fully intending to make payment for the abortion of her second child.

"The receptionist tried several times to put it through," she remembers, "but for some reason it wouldn't work. The machine wouldn't accept the card."

What do you do when you're standing at the cashier's desk, half dressed, nurses waiting impatiently to escort you to the abortion table, and you can't come up with the money to pay for the service? Adrienne felt confused and frustrated—and at that moment happened to look down the stairway leading to the procedure room.

A sense of horror and dread suddenly gripped her.

"I just got this overwhelming feeling that if I went down there I would not come back upstairs alive, that I would literally die in this place if I didn't leave right now. I remember grabbing Clint's arm, grabbing the card, grabbing my shirt, and literally running for my life out of that clinic."

Clint's friends were understandably concerned that the card could not be processed. It was their only credit card and they needed it to pay bills and make purchases. But they needn't have feared; the next day they put a $600 purchase on it with no problems whatsoever. "I definitely think that the hand of

God was involved in saving both my son's life and my own life that day," says Adrienne.

She gave birth to Justin in February of the following year. "Growing up, I was never one of those girls who liked kids," she recalls. "I never wanted kids of my own, never baby-sat for other people's kids, so I had no frame of reference from which to understand what it's like to have children in the house."

She had to learn. Fast. "I've been forced to grow up much faster than I ever would have if I hadn't had a child. I've been forced to make adult decisions, to make responsible decisions, to quit making selfish decisions."

That spring she returned to participate in graduation with the rest of her senior class. The experience painfully reminded her how quickly and drastically her life had changed. "I recall that as one of the worst days I had. I walked into graduation and all of the seniors were milling around, waiting to walk. A group of guys—most of them had been pretty close friends of mine in high school—came over to where I was standing with some of my friends. One of them looked at me and said, 'What are *you* doing here? Don't you know you're not one of us anymore?'"

That was a brand of rejection Adrienne had never known. Until that year, her life had revolved almost exclusively around her friends. Now she watched those same friends climbing into cars to celebrate with their classmates . . . while she went home, a smile on her face and a sinking feeling in the pit of her stomach, to a small party with her parents, her sisters, and her four-month-old son.

Today Adrienne's whole world revolves around that little boy and his moment-to-moment needs. "It's ideal if he takes an afternoon nap so I have an hour or two to study. But if he's sick, or if he's just really hyper and doesn't feel like taking a nap, then my plans for that afternoon change. I play with him and I'm with him. Everything I do centers around making sure his needs get met. I don't really have any friends. There's nobody that I hang out with other than my family and Justin—nobody that I can call on the phone and talk to. So I definitely feel lonely a lot."

And then there's her *other* child. The one she never knew.

Sometimes, when she looks at Justin, Adrienne can't help thinking of the daughter she never had a chance to hold; the little girl she has since christened Gracie Kathleen. Gracie's memory lives on in the form of a teddy bear with the same name. Adrienne takes that bear with her whenever she goes into school classrooms to talk to students

about the importance of saving sex for marriage—something she does regularly because
she so desperately wants to help teens avoid
the mistakes she made.

"I look at my little Gracie bear," she says,
"and I see my little girl. It makes it very real
that there was a life, that there were arms
that, maybe, could have held that bear had I
let her live. That has to be something that I
block out most of the time. It would be too
overwhelmingly painful if I allowed myself
to think about that every day—about the fact
that there was a child growing inside of me,
and I chose to let that child die because I was
selfish and young and scared and stupid and
worried about me and my own best interests. That little girl never had a chance to
smile or to laugh, to hold my hand. She's
gone."

"No Idea ..."

In her work with Care for the Family in
the U.K., Joanna Thompson has counseled
with hundreds of young women with stories
just like Adrienne's—and Leslie's and
Sarah's. Joanna has seen the familiar patterns
surface over and over again. She has heard
the tape replayed so often that she can
almost recite it by heart. Experience and
observation have given her a keen insight

into the difficulties and dilemmas many teens face in the area of sexual activity.

"I was a teenager in the '60s," says Joanna. "That's when the whole message of 'free love' really came into vogue. We thought we had found freedom. All I can say is that when I see young couples, young teenagers who come into our counseling room and sit on the sofa, they have not found freedom. We have sold them a lie. We have said that free love, free sex, brings freedom. It doesn't. It brings problems. It brings difficulties. It brings the opposite to freedom. These young people aren't free.

"Young people who buy into this lie have no idea what they're playing with," she adds. "They have no idea of the consequences."

8
Redirection

In his book *Pure Excitement*, Joe White reproduces the following letter from a young lady named Diane. Diane was only 14 years old when she recounted the story of her experience with premarital sex.

> I slept with a guy. I'd known him for a long time but hadn't seen him in a while. When we saw each other, we both noticed each other. He was good friends with my older brother, so he'd come over a lot. Every time he came over, we would flirt and talk a lot. My family joked with me and said we liked each other, but I always denied it.

One day, my family went out of town and left me at home. Someone was staying with me, but she didn't get to my house until late that night. My brother's friends (like four of them) stayed at the house to look out for me. After everyone left, that one guy came back. We kissed and "messed around," then he left. But he started calling me. Every time he came over, we would somehow end up alone. We would talk and laugh and kiss. He made a remark about how I should sneak out and come to his house. Being only fourteen, I thought that would be cool, so one night I did.

I didn't plan on having sex with him, but one thing led to another, and I did. I told him I didn't want to, but he said, "You know you're going to do it, so would you rather do it with me or would you rather it be someone else?" I thought for a second and still said no, but when he wouldn't give up, I just went for it. I thought I'd end up doing it anyway, so I might as well do it with someone I knew real well. We still talked and were friends, and a few weeks later, I snuck out again and slept with him again. We remained friends for a few weeks, then some people found out, and we stopped talking to each other.

I saw him recently when I was out with my friends; I said, "Hi." He said the same, then he introduced me to his girlfriend, but not with my name. He called me "Matt's little sister." I thought, When do I get my name? When will I stop being the "little sister"? I knew then how shallow and foolish the whole thing was.

I deeply regret what I did. I've made a promise to myself and God that I will never do it again. I've made my boundaries so I'll never do anything like that again. God has forgiven me, and I'm a spiritual virgin again. Although this is my second virginity, it will be with me until I'm married.[1]

Diane found out—to her sorrow—that the power of sexuality was something she *should* have handled more thoughtfully and intentionally. She got caught without a plan, without a strategy for dealing with the pressure. Like Adrienne and Sarah and Leslie and so many of the others we've met, Diane found herself doing something she hadn't planned to do and never meant to do.

Just because "one thing led to another."

But Diane's hollow and hurtful experience also led to another discovery. It brought her to the place where she could see, maybe for the first time, that God really is a God of grace and forgiveness. She found out that, with Him, it's *always* possible to start over—that He is the God of new beginnings. And she laid hold of that truth and made it her own by doing something brave and decisive: She made a commitment to be smarter about sex in the future—to save herself for the man who would someday be her husband. It's *never* too late to take that step.

Eyes on the Goal

> *Teens today are uncommitted…I know a lot of people just go for whatever's there at the moment. They don't have a goal.*
> —Molly (15)

Ever played darts? No one hits the bull's eye every time. But if you *aim* at the bull's eye, there's a pretty good chance you'll at least hit the board!

A lot of single people, both teens and

adults, are saying that abstinence is an unattainable ideal; that it's unrealistic to expect them to wait until marriage before climbing into bed with the one they love (or *think* they love). Maybe it *is* hard, especially in the midst of today's sex-saturated culture. But it's also possible that this attitude proves an old saying: "Aim low and you'll hit the mark every time."

"I would say it's hard to abstain," says Jack, "because I've been exposed to sex a lot. You know, it's in all the movies. It's on television."

Mark agrees. "I personally believe it's just almost impossible to abstain," he says.

"I think it is kind of difficult to stay a virgin as a teenager because there is a lot of peer pressure out there to do those types of things," suggests Matt.

"Adults know that teens are going to have sex…and that they can't help it." That's Maggie's opinion. "So the only thing they can do about it is help kids prevent getting diseases and things like that."

What do *you* think? Are these statements a fair assessment of *your* ability to control your own actions and make smart decisions? Or could it be that Jack and Mark and Matt and Maggie have been shooting at the wrong target? Thought and behavior have a way of gravitating toward the lodestone of previously established standards and expectations.

Michelle Baranek would like to raise the bar several notches. She believes teenagers are every bit equal to a higher calling and a stiffer challenge. "It isn't easy being a teen today. But kids *can* abstain. These are not animals we're talking about. They're human beings who can make moral decisions and follow through on those decisions—especially if they're given the tools and skills to do that."

Michelle is right. And the people who keep telling us that it's unrealistic to talk about saving intercourse for marriage are wrong. It *is* possible to abstain from sexual activity outside of marriage. Not only is it possible, it's a rational, reasonable, and realistic way for human beings to live. And the first step toward turning that possibility into an actuality is to set your sights on the goal. Make purity your aim. Decide now to save yourself for marriage. Establish a fixed, immovable set of standards *before* you find yourself in a tempting or compromising situation. You'll be surprised what a little intelligent self-determination can do.

Let's take a closer look at the goal we have in mind—and just exactly how it can be achieved.

The Vision of Marriage

> *What we want to do at our seminars is to give kids a really big vision for sex. A really big vision for love, bigger than they've ever heard of or seen before.*
> —Eva Ashburn

"Without a vision," the old prophet said, "the people perish."

So dare to dream big. If you can picture it, you're halfway there.

That's the first truth to lay hold of if you're serious about sexual purity. If you're convinced that abstinence is an impossible ideal, you won't have much motivation to stay out of bed before marriage. But if you can see it in your mind's eye and look beyond the present to that moment in the future when sex, love, and committed marriage will come together in your life like the three strands of a strong and sturdy rope, you may find the goal easier to reach than you had imagined.

What's *your* picture of marriage? What's the rule you use to measure and define family life? Think about it for a minute, and then take note of this: Whether you know it or not, you *will* be drawn toward your own standard. Positive or negative, your vision of marriage and family is going to attract you like a magnet. If you think it has to be a certain way, then it's likely to turn out that way for you. That's why it's so important to gain a positive, healthy vision of sex and marriage—the vision of what they were meant to be, and still *can* be, in God's perfect plan.

"Wait a minute," someone will say. "You don't know *my* parents. You didn't grow up in *my* home. Let me tell you how much it hurts. I've watched my mom and dad, two people who said they'd love each other 'til death do us part,' fight and scratch and claw and wound one another. I've seen their 'permanent' relationship scrapped and tossed on the garbage heap. Don't talk to me about 'a vision for marriage.' I've got good reasons for wanting to keep the fun of sex completely separate from the misery of marriage."

Viewed from that perspective, abstinence isn't just difficult—it's pointless. Why save sex for marriage if marriage is something you've decided to avoid at all costs? If that's your point of view, you won't even want to *discuss* the subject of sexual purity during the teen years. But if you, like Diane, have seen the other side of the coin—if you've experienced the emptiness of premarital intercourse and reached the painful conclusion that there *has* to be a better way—then the first thing you need is to get a firm grasp of what you *really* want.

You need to see that sex *is* for marriage and that marriage does not have to be the nightmare you've been led to believe it is. If you can dream of something better, you'll begin to desire it. And once you have the desire, you'll find yourself doing whatever it takes to achieve it. Suddenly, you'll possess a powerful motive for staying pure.

So what if your home life hasn't equipped you with the best example of married love? That doesn't mean that good models don't exist. Search out someone whose experience has been different—an adult friend, a pastor, or a youth leader—someone who can help you get hold of a clearer, more attractive vision of what love, sex, and marriage are meant to be. There are plenty of people like that out there...people like Mike and Eva Ashburn.

Eva points out that most of the teen girls she works with are hungry not for "discon-nected" sex, but for a relationship marked by love, sensitivity, and commitment—a place where sex is entered into within a larger con-text of "belonging." That, in her experience, is what marriage is all about.

"You won't find what we're talking about

in a romance novel," says Eva. "It's like Ash says: Sex doesn't begin at night when we get in bed together. It begins in the morning when he comes up and gives me a hug at the sink. That's what the girls I talk to are searching for."

"It's sad that teenagers today aren't really getting that tender, wholesome message," adds Ash. "When the topic of sex comes up, the focus immediately shifts to STDs, AIDS, and pregnancy. It would be wonderful if teens could hear about this other side of sex, like writing your wife a love letter or giving her a hug just because you love her; to be dreaming and imagining themselves in that situation...picturing marriage in terms of love and tenderness."

Imagine it. A 50-plus-year love life. A partnership where two companions never stop learning what it means to become "one" at every level of their existence; where they're always figuring out new ways to put the other person first, to please one another, to deepen mutual affection; where every day presents another opportunity to lay selfishness aside, to treat your partner with gentle sensitivity, to discover something about that other person you had somehow missed. To learn and practice and perfect the art of love.

It isn't Fantasyland. It's as real as this

morning's sunrise. It's an everyday reality for countless marriages.

Joe White is enthusiastic about helping teens develop what he calls "Great Sexpectations." He knows what he's talking about—his own marriage models the concept. "I've been married 25 years," says Joe, "and holding my bride's hand and kissing her tenderly is still more satisfying, dearly affectionate, and fun than it was the time before. My wife is fantastic. I love her more today than I did the day I slipped the diamond ring into the surprise packet in the Cracker Jack box I handed her while atop a beautiful Ozark mountain 25 years ago!"

Picture it. If you can, you're halfway there.

Laying a Foundation: Know Yourself

> *I'm proud to be a virgin and I know that I'm saving myself for my husband...The benefits for me are that I will be pure and I will have something to look forward to when I get married.*
> —Allison (13)

But how do you finish the journey? Is there anything you can do *now* to begin laying a foundation for what Joe White calls the "indescribable splendor" of God's design for a man and a woman within the bonds of marriage? Or is it all a matter of waiting for that exciting day when you and Mr. or Miss Right stand before the altar and repeat your vows?

As a matter of fact, there is a great deal you can do—even if you don't have a boyfriend or girlfriend and aren't currently in the market for one. And the first thing you can do is spend some quality time getting to know yourself. It's what Michelle Baranek calls "the whole person approach."

"Self-sufficiency," she says, "is a crucial component of the 'whole person approach.' Not only should you be self-sufficient emotionally, but physically, intellectually, socially, and spiritually. You should be able to provide for all of your needs in all of those areas or at least know of resources to do that." In other words, work to get yourself to the point where you can stand alone and say, "I know who I am and where I'm going, and I'm happy about it." Only then will you be ready to share yourself, body and soul, with another person.

As part of this process you might want to take some time to write down a list of everything that's important to you regarding sex, marriage, and family. Try to look at sex as it relates to and fits in with everything you are and everything you hope to be. Put it into the context of the bigger picture of your life. Prioritize. Ask yourself which is more important—family, friends, self-esteem, mental and physical health, academic achievement, career goals...or a stolen moment of sexual pleasure?

Stacy was 16 when she heard the challenge to rethink her priorities. It changed her attitude toward sex—and turned her life around.

"I went to church with a friend," she says, "and the minister was talking about premarital sex. I thought I was going to get reamed because I was sexually active back then. Instead, the minister talked about all the good things God wanted for my life— and why he wanted me to wait to have sex. I started crying because I realized that God loved me more than I loved myself. That was the turning point!"[2]

"When I was a teenager," observes Leslie, "I was just becoming who I was going to be—just little hints and glimpses into who I would be as an adult, as a wife and mother. Just starting. But when I became pregnant, it all stopped...I had to live on my high school education and whatever maturity I had attained up to that point." And that's no way to enter a marriage—as Leslie will be the first to tell you.

Taking Things in Order

The second thing you can do—especially if you think you've found your "special someone"—is to realize that a long-lasting, deeply satisfying marriage depends on the strength and quality of the bonds that form between two people *before* they make an irrevocable commitment to one another. According to researcher Dr. Desmond Morris, that bonding process is a precise and delicate thing. It's like building a model airplane: You have to follow the instructions, take each step in order, and allow the glue to dry before moving on to the next operation. If you don't, you run the risk of watching your work fall to pieces before your very eyes.

Dr. Morris says there are 12 stages of marital bonding. He names each of these stages after the physical expression of love that best represents it. Only eight of the steps are appropriate to the premarital stage of a relationship: *eye to body, eye to eye, voice to voice, hand to hand, hand to shoulder, hand to waist, face to face,* and *hand to head.* The most successful marriages, says Dr. Morris, are those where the couples involved took these steps slowly and in order during their courtship—and saved the last four stages, *hand to body, mouth to breast, touching below the waist,* and *sexual intercourse,* for their wedding night.

Here's the important point. If steps are skipped, scrambled, substituted for one another, or rushed into too soon—for example, if a boy and girl kiss passionately on their first date, engage in heavy petting a month after getting acquainted, or have sexual intercourse before marriage—the relationship suffers.

Something precious is lost, perhaps beyond recovery. Self-respect and respect for one's partner is damaged, the magic of romance is trampled, and the "glue" isn't given a chance to dry. The result? A rising divorce rate and an increasingly negative vision of marriage in the minds of many people.

"Time is the critical ingredient," writes Dr. James Dobson. There's real wisdom in his words, a wisdom that true lovers can't afford to ignore.

To put it more simply: If you want a deeply fulfilling marriage with your future mate—if you want to go the distance and weather the storms of life together—don't "get physical" too soon. *And stay out of bed until you're married.*

Devising a Plan of Action

> *The decision not to have sexual intercourse should be made long before the opportunity presents itself.*
>
> —Dr. James Dobson,
> *Life on the Edge*

Easy to say, right? A good idea. But… how? Exactly *how* do you confront sexual temptation when it comes knocking at your door? Here are some practical suggestions.

1. *Set high standards—in advance.*

Just how far is too far? Good question. And it's one you need to answer before you find yourself in the back seat of a car, in the arms of someone who claims to be madly in love with you and whom you find irresistibly attractive. At that point, it's probably too late to step back and analyze the situation objectively.

"Set your standards higher than you need to," says Joshua Harris, a single who "kissed dating good-bye" and lived to write a book about it. "Physical interaction encourages us to start something we're not supposed to finish…. The wrong use of our sexuality is like a highway to the grave. We

174

shouldn't get on it, then try to stop before we arrive at the destination—God tells us to stay off that highway completely."[3]

"It's important for me to know where the stopping point is," says Alice, 17. "I need to make that judgment so I don't get myself into a situation that I won't be able to handle…. I once had a boyfriend who wanted more than I did. I let him know where I stood as far as my morals, my beliefs, and he took it okay."

Just how far is too far? That's the million-dollar question, isn't it? You can argue that each of us is different, that "too far" for me isn't the same as "too far" for you. But when it comes right down to it, we all know—at least while we're in our right minds—when we've crossed that critical line, tossed concern for another person's best interests to the winds, and shifted into the self-gratification mode. That's the definition of "lust," and *that's* going too far.

"How far is too far?" asks Joe. "Getting into the state of mind where you want to 'do it.'"

Dr. James Dobson, who is reluctant to create a set of strict rules and regulations, does suggest the following guidelines for keeping physical desires under control: "A very early decision must be made to delay kissing, fondling, caressing, and other forms of physical contact. Failure to put the relationship on a slower timetable may result in an act that was never intended …. A girl who wants to preserve her virginity should not find herself in a house or dorm room alone with someone to whom she is attracted. Nor should she single-date with someone she has no reason to trust. A guy who wants to be moral should stay away from the girl he knows would go to bed with him."[4]

And Mike Ashburn has a special word of caution for the guys: "I'd especially like to tell young men that touching is a big, *big* deal. I'm just wondering if guys don't realize that they have her very soul in their hands. In general, I want young couples to hear the message that kissing, hugging, and holding hands is as far as we'd recommend that people go up until they get married. *And that might be too far for some.*"

How far is too far? Don't take this question lightly. The stakes are extremely high. "I went a little too far with one of my girlfriends," remembers Paul, "and we ended up in bed. We really destroyed our relationship." So take some time *now*—before it's too late—to think about it. And if there's something you *know* you just can't handle, *decide that you will not do it.*

2. *Recognize the progressive nature of sex, and go slowly.*

This suggestion is linked to the last one. If you want to stop, you'd better do it before you've passed the point of no return. The stages leading to sexual intercourse are like a stairway that spirals downward and gets a little steeper at every step. Or, to go back to an image we employed a little earlier, sex is like a rapid river. Anyone who is serious about remaining abstinent is going to have to stay out of the current. If you rush too quickly through those steps of physical bonding you'll find yourself downstream— and over the falls—before you know what hit you.

One study indicated that when a couple has been together for approximately 300 hours, even most of those who are trying to hold themselves to a standard of sexual purity will end up doing things they hadn't intended.[5] By that point, they've reached a place where hand-holding or an occasional good-night kiss aren't as exciting as they were in the beginning. If nothing happens to interrupt the natural flow of things, they'll become more physical week by week until they find themselves in bed.

That's simply the power of sex.

"Next time you go for a drive," says Joe

White, "notice how the automatic transmission shifts from one gear to the next. Step on the gas and it sails smoothly from low gear to second, from second to drive, and from drive to overdrive in a matter of seconds. *That's* what petting does with sex. It's an automatic transmission to intercourse."[6]

Better figure out how to put on the brakes before you've gone too far. Singer Rebecca St. James gets the point: "I've kind of got the mentality that I'm just going to be friends with guys for a while," she says. "I'm going to take it slowly."

3. *Guard your heart and mind.*

Rebecca has also thought—and prayed—hard about outside influences. "One thing God has really convicted me about is watching what I put into my mind," she says. "TV, you know, and the music we listen to. However much we like to say it doesn't affect us, it does. So I'm really careful about what I watch, because if I see everyone on television having sex, sure, I'll want to do it. Instead, I want to fill my mind with things that will encourage me to stand for God and live right."

As a recording artist, Rebecca has reason to understand just how powerfully mind-shaping the media can be. It's not just idle talk when she refers to the importance of nurturing a healthy thought-life. In the book *Chart Watch* (referenced in Chapter 2), author Bob Smithouser illustrates this point with a story of his two pet iguanas.

Liberty and Justice (so Bob dubbed them) shared the same terrarium, drank the same water, and basked in the light of the same heat lamp. Their lives were identical in every particular except for one thing: diet. "While Liberty consumed fruit, vegetables, and various forms of protein, Justice was a very picky eater with a meager appetite." The outcome? Liberty grew big and strong, the undisputed ruler of the 55-gallon tank the two lizards called home. Justice eventually died.[7]

The story of Liberty and Justice parallels our ability to live up to the challenge of sexual purity. Those aspects of our human nature that we feed and nurture will thrive and grow and eventually dominate. Those we neglect will wither and fade away like forgotten flowers. Beef up the lustful, the selfish, the sensuous side of the subconscious mind with erotic images and sexually explicit lyrics, and you'll have a hard time keeping it in check when the moon is high and the time seems right. On the other hand, spend time developing your better impulses—love for God and others, patience, self-control, compassion, and zeal for the truth—and you may be surprised at the kind of wisdom and maturity you'll be able to call on when you approach potentially compromising situations. Anyone who seriously desires to steer clear of premarital sex knows it's a matter of pressing urgency.

"Above all else," advises Solomon, "guard your heart, for it is the wellspring of life" (Proverbs 4:23). And Paul, in his letter to the Philippians, writes, "Whatever is true, whatever is noble, whatever is right, whatever is pure, whatever is lovely, whatever is admirable—if anything is excellent or praiseworthy—*think about such things*" (Philippians 4:8, emphasis added).

Our actions have their beginning in our thought life. So if you want to save yourself for the man or woman who will one day share your life, you need to close the door of your mind to messages that weaken your resolve.

4. *Question the "Dating Game."*

Dating has become a standard feature of adolescent life in America. It's almost expected. Just part of the culture. But anybody who is serious about sexual abstinence needs to take a closer look at this accepted and time-honored institution. Many are beginning to say that it may not deserve the support and respect it's been so universally accorded.

It's difficult to avoid the conclusion that single dating is basically a setup. A guy and a girl, alone together, at night, in a car—could anyone come up with a better recipe for sexual activity? As one dad said to his son, "At your age, I wouldn't have trusted *myself!* Why should I trust *you*?"

And there's something else to bear in mind. Times have changed drastically since teenage dating first came into vogue. Expectations are different. In the fifties, when a guy picked a girl up at her front door, their mutual assumptions usually went no further than a hamburger, a shake, and a movie. Nowadays, that same guy often takes it for granted that there will be some kind of sexual "payoff" at the end of the evening. That's why "date rape" has become so disturbingly common. Against *that* backdrop, it's hard to see how single dating makes sense for anyone determined to save sex for marriage.

And what about some of the other destructive effects of the dating game? Like the way it divides a group into two distinct and unmixable categories—the "desirables" and the "rejects"? The dating system favors the "beautiful people" and leaves everyone else feeling like human refuse. And that, too, is a formula for disaster, since it's often low self-esteem that leads kids to jump into premarital sex in a quest for love and significance.

"Teenage sex," conjectures Liz, "may be the result of wanting to be loved."

Julie sees the same thing: "I think some kids are insecure," she says, "and they believe that sex will take their problems away."

It can also be argued that dating creates an artificial environment for evaluating your partner's character. It tends to be a kind of game, where both players jockey for position and keep the less desirable facets of their personalities carefully out of sight. There's a dangerous phoniness about many dating relationships. They tend to isolate couples from the wider world of social interaction and lure them into an unhealthy, inward focus. Dating minimizes the importance of full-fledged friendship and distorts the true meaning of love. As Dr. James Dobson puts it, "A dating relationship is designed to *conceal* information, not reveal it."[8]

"Is this the answer?" asks Josh Harris. "Head out on the same course as those who have fallen and hope that in the critical moment you'll be able to stay in control?...I don't think so." That's why Josh, who values sexual purity enough to be extreme about it, has rejected typical dating. He wants something better.[9]

Maybe he's onto something. Maybe it's time to come up with some creative alternatives to single dating. Group dating, for example, is a great way to spend time with the opposite sex while avoiding the more threatening aspects of a one-on-one encounter.

"Be friends," suggests Rebecca St. James. "Go out in groups. There's more fun in groups, anyway, because there's a lot less pressure. You can really get to know what people are like, and I like that...I don't really enjoy traditional dating."

Some teens and their parents prefer an even more radical approach. In some circles the trend is growing to handle guy-girl relationships according to the "courtship" model. "Much sexual temptation today," says Randy Alcorn of Eternal Perspective Ministries, "is created by our social practice of coupling and isolating young people instead of doing what many other cultures have done—requiring that single people spend time together only in a context supervised by parents and other adults."[10]

Jim Ryun is a Congressman and former track star. During the late '60s and early '70s Jim held world records in the 880-yard and 1500-meter runs. He and his wife Anne have four grown (or nearly grown) children. The Ryuns have put the courtship idea into practice with great success. Dad, Mom, even brothers and sisters take an active role in screening potential companions for the members of the younger generation. Everyone involved understands that the process is something more than just a game. Any "courting" relationship could lead to marriage; in fact, marriage is always the unstated goal. For that reason, it should be taken seriously.

Courtship is founded upon the idea that romance grows healthiest when it's nurtured within the broader social context of family and friends. That, after all, is where the relationship must fit and function if it ripens and finds fulfillment in marriage. Courtship is about openness, honesty, and interconnection—about people getting to know each other in their "setting" and enjoying one another as they really are.

"Any young man who is interested in my daughter Heather," says Jim Ryun, "is going to be coming over to dinner a lot. He's going to be playing basketball with my sons. He's going to be getting acquainted with our family because we feel it's important that each member of the family have an opportunity to offer their observations about his character."

And Heather? She thinks it's a great idea. "Having family involved is important. I've learned through experience that my brothers will pick up on things that I won't pick up on, and I've learned to listen to them."

Courtship can be a great way to avoid temptation and give relationships with the opposite sex the care and respect they deserve. But even if you prefer the traditional dating model, it's still possible to make use of some of the principles of courtship. Josh Harris suggests that the following five attitude changes will help us enjoy what he calls "principled romance":

- View every relationship as an opportunity to model Christ's love.
- Accept singleness as a gift from God.
- Understand that intimacy is the reward of commitment.
- Realize that you cannot own someone outside of marriage.
- Avoid situations that could compromise purity.[11]

The bottom line? Every "date" is a potential mate and should be treated accordingly. "You should think of the person you date as someone you might spend the rest of your life with," says Molly, "because you never know."

Don't date anyone you couldn't or wouldn't marry. If you're a Christian, don't date non-Christians. Involve your parents in your dating decisions. Bring your "special someone" home to spend time with your family as often as possible. And always remember that, even if your date doesn't become *your* mate, he or she will probably marry somebody else someday. So treat that person as you'd like your future spouse to be treated.

5. *Make yourself accountable.*

Accountability is one of the courtship model's greatest strengths. But you don't have to be "courting" to keep yourself answerable to others. Find people you can talk to about the sexual temptations, pressures, and challenges you're facing—if not your own parents, then an aunt or uncle, a teacher or youth pastor, or some other adult you can trust. Get them to "keep tabs" on you and ask you how things are going from time to time. "My family and I are very open about the topic of sex," says Rebecca St. James. "They don't mind talking about it, and I want to talk about it with them because I think it's something we need to be open about."

Don't listen to that little voice that tells you no one cares, that no one will listen. You probably have no idea how many people love you and are really concerned about your well-being. And talking to someone—anyone—can make a huge difference. Just ask Leslie.

"One of the things I would change about my experience," she says, "is that I would never cut myself off from my friends. I didn't realize it, but they were really there trying to help me all along. They told me I was spending too much time with my boyfriend. They wanted to tell me what was going on. It was like they could see it but I couldn't—and I didn't listen to them. I wish I had told one adult about the pressure I was under."

6. *Use reminders.*

Anything that reminds you of your decision to hold to a high standard and save sex for marriage—a bracelet or a ring or a piece of paper bearing a written and signed promise or pledge and tucked inside your wallet or purse—can be an incalculable help and comfort to you in difficult situations. As a physical symbol of your commitment, it's something you can point to, something you can pull out and show your boyfriend or girlfriend when you're out on a hot date and feel that sexual pressure has you up against the wall. It can literally come to your rescue.

Rebecca feels strongly about this method of keeping herself on the right track. "One of the neat reminders I have is my purity ring. It reminds me of the commitment I've made to wait and not have sex before marriage. My parents presented it to me on the day I made that pledge. One day I'll probably give it to my husband. It's kind of like 'What Would Jesus Do?'—a reminder to think before I act.

"I encourage people to have that physical reminder to wait. You don't necessarily have to go out to a Christian bookstore and buy one, although they do have them. Any ring will do, as long as you remember the commitment it symbolizes."

7. *Change your peer group.*

If peer pressure is a problem, there's a pretty simple solution: Find a new group of people to hang out with. It won't be the end of your life; in fact, it might turn out to be the beginning.

Remember Adrienne? Her high school friends took sexual activity for granted. As a result, she never thought about whether it would be good or bad to lose her virginity before marriage. No one had ever told her—

or showed her by example—that it's okay not to have sex.

"I think it depends on who you hang around with," says Maggie. To a large extent, she's right. There is strength in numbers. The idea that "everybody else is doing it" can be intimidating, but if you change your social group, you may begin to see that it's nothing but a myth.

"Knowing that other people say no helps me to say no," says Allison.

"I believe that when other people say no, it encourages me to say no, too," agrees Matt.

And they *are* saying no. Rebecca hears from them all the time—guys and girls who feel that they're "the only one" taking a stand for purity—and she lets them know they have lots of company. "'You're not alone,' I tell them. 'There are thousands of teenagers out there taking the same stand as you.'"

There really are. So find them and get to know them. As Rebecca says, "We're not alone. Let's stick together!"

9

A Thousand Ways (and a Thousand Reasons) to Say "No"

Well, you may be thinking, *all of this may sound great in theory, but sometimes you just find yourself in a place you never intended to be.* A young man in the Bible named Joseph found himself in just such a situation. He was in the right place doing the right things for the right reasons, when suddenly he found himself cornered by the boss's wife—who had something more on her mind than the weather. (Read Genesis chapter 39 for the whole story.)

For Joseph, the time for conversation had ended. He let his feet do the talking and got out of the room and out of the house. *Fast.*

Fleeing an almost-out-of-control sexual

situation is always an option, and sometimes the best option of all. But whether you run or stay around to reason, it brings up a critically important question: What *can* you do when circumstances get the better of you? How do you put on the brakes when you sense your automatic transmission shifting into a higher gear? Girls especially would be well advised to have a strategy in place—and to drill themselves in it—before they find themselves falling under the spell of some charming guy who has rehearsed all the right lines…and knows how to use them.

Paul Simon, rock poet of the '60s and '70s, once had a hit song called "(There must be) Fifty Ways to Leave Your Lover." Simon had it wrong; there are far more ways than that. Actually, the possibilities are endless.

You would be extremely wise to arm yourself with an arsenal of refusal skills, and take some time to practice them (you can role-play with a friend).

"What can I do to cool off a hot date?" asks Allison. "I can say no. I can walk away. I can tell him I'm not interested, or that I only want to be his friend—or that I don't want to know him at all!"

"I'd suggest that we take a walk," says Alice, "or see what's on TV. Or play a game. Change the surroundings, maybe. I wouldn't want to be in a house all alone with my boyfriend."

"Run away!" says Rebecca St. James. (That's what Joseph did.) "The Bible talks about 'fleeing'—just not hanging around where you could possibly be tempted to sin."

"If I could go back to that moment in time," reflects Leslie, "I would find one person to coach me, to help me with my refusal skills. I'd do whatever I could to find my way out of a bad situation. I would continue to say no. I would get myself prepared to say no in a *final* way, and I would risk this guy walking away from me."

It might help to write down some of the lines you've heard, then try to come up with a few witty responses. It's good for a few laughs—and they *could* come in handy in a pinch. Here are a few examples to help you get started:

Line: *Sex will make our relationship better.*
Response: *No it won't. It will become the center of attention and ruin our relationship.*

Line: *I'll be careful. I know when to stop.*
Response: *So do I. Like right now.*

Line: *We'll get married someday.*

Response: *Good. We'll pick up this conversation then.*

Line: *Don't be so uptight!*
Response: *Don't be so selfish!*

Line: *We love each other, so that makes it all right.*
Response: *Love doesn't make demands.*

Line: *Sex will bring us closer together.*
Response: *Our bodies, you mean.*

Line: *I want to give you something to remember me by.*
Response: *Like maybe a disease?*

Line: *We've already had sex. Why don't you want to now?*
Response: *I guess I've learned something from my mistakes.*

Line: *You try on shoes before you buy them, don't you?*
Response: *Yeah, and you walk all over them, too.*

Line: *If you love me, you'll show me.*
Response: *If you love me, you'll show me some respect.*

Line: *Don't worry, I've got protection.*
Response: *So do I. It's called "saying no," and it works every time.*

Line: *Nobody will know.*
Response: *I will.*

Line: *It's our anniversary. It's special.*
Response: *It will be even more special if we wait for our wedding night.*

Line: *We don't have to go all the way.*
Response: *I don't, but you do. All the way out the door.*

Line: *I can't stop now. You've gotten me all excited!*
Response: *Oh, look! Here comes my dad!*

Line: *If you won't, I'll find someone who will.*
Response: *I hope the two of you have a very nice life together.*

Pray for Strength and Perseverance

Okay, but what happens when you've practiced your lines, studied your strategies, protected yourself in every way you can think of, and you *still* feel vulnerable? Listen, that may be good news. If you sense that you haven't yet arrived (and who has?), that you're still open to peer pressure, media influence, and other forms of sexual enticement, remember this: an awareness of your own weakness *can* be the first step in the right direction. It's the guy or girl who thinks he or she is "above temptation" who stands in the greatest danger. Pride goes before a fall.

If you *know* you're weak—or even if you think you *might* be weak in certain situations—don't hesitate to let God be your strength. He has promised to defend everyone who looks to Him for guidance and cries out to Him for help. "No temptation has seized you except what is common to man. And God is faithful; he will not let you be tempted beyond what you can bear. But when you are tempted, he will also provide a way out so that you can stand up under it" (1 Corinthians 10:13).

"He [Jesus] had to be made like his brothers [us] in every way...," says the writer of Hebrews. "Because he himself suffered when he was tempted, he is able to help those who are being tempted" (Hebrews 2:17-18). So ask for His help and you *will* receive!

God Knows How You Feel

That leads us to our last point: If you find yourself caught in the "hormone gap"—in that crucible between your sexual desires and the standards by which you've chosen to live—*remember that you don't have to face the pressure alone*. God is with you, and He knows how you feel. He knows because He designed you that way. What's more, in Jesus Christ He has experienced those same feelings and emotions Himself. (And He was also a teenager!) Allison has done a great job of putting that thought into words.

"I think God knows exactly how it feels to have hormones and stuff," she says, "because He's the one who created them, and He also had Jesus come down to earth to be a human being. I'm sure Jesus felt all those feelings when He was down here."

"Recycled Virgins"

> *I really, truly believe that there is hope and forgiveness for people who have already made the decision to have sex before marriage. I really believe they can say, "From now on I will wait. I'll not have sex before marriage. In Christ I'm forgiven, and I can stand for God from now on."*
>
> —Rebecca St. James

Maybe you're thinking, *Okay, that's fine— fine for people who have kept themselves pure, preserved their virginity, and resisted every temptation to have sex before marriage. But what about me? I've already blown it. I've already messed up. And once you've given your virginity away, you can never get it back. I've been stained with permanent ink, and I'll never be the same again. So what's the use of trying anymore?*

From a certain angle—the physical, the psychological, the emotional—those statements are true. There's no denying the power of sex or the depth of the pain it can cause when misused. As in Adrienne's, Sarah's, and Leslie's experience, the consequences of sex outside of marriage are very real and often devastating. Those consequences should never be minimized or diluted.

"The promiscuity of my early adult life," writes Steve Arterburn, "—what I considered to be 'free love'—ended up costing me dearly. Because sexual sin involves intense intimacy between two humans, it almost always has enduring consequences…. Like a virus that 'disappears' and then re-emerges to cause more painful symptoms, my sexual sin has been a source of deep and often unexpected trouble."

Sexual mistakes are costly. It's certainly not the purpose of this book to suggest they don't matter. Far from it! We *do* have to live with the results of our actions and choices. But—and this is the good news—that's not the end of the story. There's more to life than its physical, psychological, and emotional facets. At the bottom of everything is the *spiritual* element, that place in our hearts, at the very core of our being, where we are known by God and have the capacity to know and love Him.

That spiritual element provides the foundation of our existence and the key to who we really are. *That's* where we can be reborn, washed clean, and given a completely new start. *That's* where we can tap into the miracle-working power of God's renewing forgiveness and grace. So if you've made a mistake, take heart: He is ready, willing, and able to wipe away your tears *and* the stains of your errors and give you a fresh start. In that sense, you *can* become a virgin again—a recycled or secondary virgin. What an exciting idea!

"Imagine this," says Mike Ashburn. "You've put on a brand-spanking-new, clean white shirt and gone to a party or a wedding reception. Everybody's looking at that shirt and noticing how clean and white and unstained it is. They're all oohing and aahing over it and you're standing there talking with a cup of red punch in your hand—the kind that's made with cranberry juice and Kool-Aid and number 2 red dye—when suddenly you spill your drink down the front of your shirt. You do everything you can to get that stain out. You cover it up. You take it to the cleaners and they bring out their big artillery and pour every chemical and enzyme known to man all over it. But even when that shirt is as clean as it can possibly be, the stain is still visible. The shirt will never be the same.

"That's what sexual sin is like. That's what it's like to lose your virginity. But just when we've given up all hope, God, in His grace, takes that shirt from us and removes the stain. Not only does He hand it back to us totally and completely clean, He actually presents it to us in the original, unbroken wrapper. That's what His forgiveness is like. His forgiveness is total. It's like starting over."

You can start over, too. It's *never* too late. Not with God!

If you're a virgin, stay a virgin. If you've fallen, the Lord can raise you up. If you're still having sex, stop. Today is the most important day you've ever lived, because today is the day when your life can begin heading in a new direction. Trust Him to fill the empty place in your heart and make you whole again. Pray the prayer that King

David prayed after he committed sexual sin with Bathsheba: "Wash me, and I will be whiter than snow…Hide your face from my sins and blot out all my iniquity. Create in me a pure heart, O God, and renew a steadfast spirit within me" (Psalm 51:7-10). He *will* hear and answer.

"Virginity really is a gift," says Rebecca. "It's something special that God has given us to share with that one special person. And for those who have already had sex, it's always possible to become *recycled* virgins. In that way, somebody who has made that mistake can still give that gift to his or her future husband or wife."

Taking the Pledge

> *"God, I'm committed to living your way. I want to wait for my husband. I don't want to have sex before marriage, and here today I commit myself to do that."*
> —Rebecca St. James

No matter who you are or what you've done, *you* can give the gift of purity to your future husband or wife on your wedding night. Nothing can keep you from following through on your pledge. Peer pressure may be intimidating, media influence pervasive, temptations formidable, and (at times) the power of your own sexual drives nearly overwhelming. But the truth is that *no force in the universe can match the strength of your will when it's energized and empowered by the grace of God.*

The choice is yours and yours alone. All the facts in the world, all the persuasive words of all the people we've quoted in this book, all the sad stories of all the young men and women who have hurt themselves and others by engaging in sexual intercourse outside of marriage—none of it makes a bit of difference unless *you* are ready to draw some personal conclusions from the evidence and put them into practice.

And taking the pledge *does* make a difference. Just knowing that you've made such a commitment will make you stronger. Statistics prove it: A study of more than 12,000 teens done by the University of Minnesota and reported in the September, 1997 issue of the *Journal of the American Medical Association* showed that kids who take a vow of abstinence are significantly less likely to engage in premarital sexual activity than those who don't.[1] They know who they are and where they're going, and they have the strength and determination to stick to their convictions and stay the course.

Actor Austin O'Brien has taken that step and made that pledge. His words are a great model for anyone who wants to do the same:

"I'm making that commitment right now—a commitment to myself, to my future wife, to my parents, and to the kids that I hope to have some day. This way, I have a chance to accomplish all the things that I want to and to live my life without making too many apologies."

No apologies. No more regret. Now *that's* a target worth aiming at.

10

No Apologies

*So I will restore to you the years that the
swarming locust has eaten,
the crawling locust, the consuming
locust, and the chewing locust,
My great army which I sent among
    you.
You shall eat in plenty and be satisfied,
and praise the name of the LORD your
    God.*
                    —Joel 2:25-26 (NKJV)

*But by the grace of God I am what I am,
and his grace to me was not without
effect.*
                —Paul (1 Corinthians 15:10)

Amazing Grace

Is it possible to live your life without making—or expecting—too many apologies? Even if you've been hurt in ways you can never forget? Even if you've already stumbled, stepped on other people's toes, and generally made a mess of things?

The answer is . . . *yes.*

The world is a strange and wonderful place, and God's grace is a marvelous, inexplicable thing. Best of all, His forgiveness is only the *first page* of a never-ending story. The real miracle of life in Christ is that God not only *forgives* our sins and mistakes, He actually takes those dark threads and weaves them into the larger pattern of His plan for our lives and the lives of countless other people, so that the shadows mingle with the light and become an indispensable part of the picture. No one can explain it, but it's true. He really does restore the years the locust has eaten. He causes a big bouquet of bright flowers to grow out of our ash-heap lives. And He finds a way to work us *and* our mistakes into an all-encompassing design of incomprehensible subtlety and beauty. That's what He's up to . . . *all* the time. It is His specialty.

Mistakes . . . But No Coincidences

The Bible is full of stories illustrating that grand truth—stories about people whose blunders and errors somehow turned into strategic turning points in God's master plan for the good of the world. Amazingly enough, sexual sins have a way of showing up in that record and even becoming an important piece in the fabric of "the plan of salvation."

It's odd. It can leave you scratching your head. But it also has a way of making you think, *maybe there's hope for* me *after all!*

One of the easiest places to see this is in "The Begats"—those long and boring genealogical records that everybody loves to skip when they're reading through the Scriptures. Take a look, for instance, at the list of Jesus' ancestors in chapter 1 of Matthew's Gospel. Judah is one of the first to be named there: "Judah begot Perez and Zerah by Tamar" (NKJV). Sounds bland enough, right? A real yawner. But hold on. Do you know the story of Judah and Tamar? Tamar was Judah's daughter-in-law. When her husband died without leaving her any children, she tricked Judah into having sex with her by posing as a prostitute. Little Perez came along nine months later.

Perez was the great-great-great-great-grandfather of Salmon, a guy who got involved with a real prostitute—or a former prostitute, at any rate: Rahab, the woman who hid the Israelite spies and helped Joshua capture the city of Jericho. And the son of Salmon and Rahab was Boaz, great-grandfather of David the king.

David, of course, had a pretty racy story of his own. He stole another man's wife, got her pregnant, and had her husband killed. A terrible sin, but the story ends with an interesting twist. The woman, Bathsheba, became David's wife and eventually gave birth to Solomon, the grandest, wisest, most glorious, and most powerful of ancient Israel's kings.

And Solomon? Well, he had a lot of positive points, but *his* highly unusual love life proved to be his undoing. He boasted about a thousand wives and concubines, most of them foreign pagans who influenced their husband to betray his faith in the Lord and start sacrificing to idols.

That was the beginning of a long, downward slide for the nation of Israel. Solomon and his royal descendants (royal pains, some of them) kept on begetting children and sinning and messing up and missing the point and blowing it in a hundred different ways. Finally, several centuries and a Babylonian exile later, a humble man named Jacob was born into the line (we know nothing of him except his name). Jacob became the father of

Joseph; and Joseph was "the husband of Mary, by whom was born Jesus, who is called Christ."

Are sexual mistakes and indiscretions the end of the line? Apparently not, because *this* long line of shameful and embarrassing mistakes produced—surprise!—the Savior of the world.

It just goes to show that God is ready to give us much more than forgiveness for our sins. By His grace, those sins can actually be turned into stepping stones that lead to a new and better world. No need for apologies there!

Leslie: "More Valuable Than Diamonds"

Leslie's story wonderfully illustrates this principle. Leslie had reached the point of despair. She lost her former life as a happy-go-lucky high schooler, lost her innocence, lost her chance to attend college and make something of herself... even lost her ability to laugh. Stuck in a drab little apartment with a baby and a teenage husband who made her life miserable, she became suicidal. She hadn't the slightest idea what to do.

Enter a small miracle.

Someone entered Leslie's life from outside her closed and seemingly endless circle of crisis and pain: a baby-sitter, a woman in her late 40s who welcomed Leslie's son into her home when she had to work. Leslie didn't know it, but it was a turning point. A new beginning. A seed of hope.

"She was like a grandmother to my baby and an incredible inspiration to me. I honestly don't think I could have survived even the first two years of marriage without her; had it not been for her, I'm positive I would have committed suicide. She began to speak truth into my life and life into me.

"This lady began to tell me, from the first time she met with me, how incredibly special I was. She always told me I was beautiful. She said I had unique gifts and talents."

As her baby grew into an energetic toddler, Leslie's friendship with this remarkable baby-sitter also deepened and grew. "She had been working with me for almost three years, trying to get me to see myself as valuable. She talked me through the times when I wanted to kill myself, quit, or run away. She could make me stop and think just by looking into my eyes."

One day, the two of them took Leslie's son, now nearly three years old, for a walk in the park. They lingered and loitered, talking about this and that and watching the little boy as he played on the grass and in the sand. Then, suddenly, Leslie's friend stopped, turned, looked straight at her, and said, "You have such incredible worth. I want you to know that you are valuable to God."

"Valuable to God..." repeated Leslie doubtfully. "Valuable to *God?*"

"More valuable than diamonds," was the wise woman's response.

That's when Leslie gave her broken and battered heart to Jesus. She was 20 years old. It wasn't the end of all her troubles and it didn't wipe away all the effects of her bad choices. But it was a beginning. That very day, that very hour, marked the start of something wonderful and new and exciting.

"Christ came in and immediately began giving me a new life," she remembers. "And yet, the consequences of my former life didn't go away. I was still a young and inexperienced mom. I was still in a terrible marriage. I still had all the responsibilities of being stable, as stable as I could be for this little boy. But now I had someone, God, who gave me value and worth and hope that I was going to make it."

Leslie had found the hug she was looking for. The real thing. At last!

And she *did* make it. In time she found the strength and determination to escape the dysfunctional relationship that began with such promise but ended by threatening to destroy her. "I left my husband after nine years of marriage. It was very difficult—a decision I couldn't have made on my own. Years and years of battering and abuse had taken away my ability to think for myself. I was in acute depression. But some very close friends at my church rescued me and my children (two of them by now). They drove me to another state and brought me to a family who took care of me for about four months until I was in a state of mind to understand what was happening. It probably took another year after that before I got back my basic personality, my will to live, and the ability to take responsibility for myself as an adult."

With the help of Christian friends, Leslie began to rebuild her life on a foundation of hope and healing. She still had more than her fair share of challenges and obstacles to overcome. "I worked very hard to be a good mother. I didn't want to be the statistic: a teenage parent who didn't take care of her kid, who ended up in the social services office. I got involved in every single school activity and my little boy came to be known as a bright young man. He became a great athlete and went on to make his mom very proud."

That boy's high school graduation marked

an important milestone along the road to Leslie's recovery. She'll never forget that day—"an odd, odd day," she muses. "It was like we had come full circle. My son had been at *my* high school graduation, and here I was sitting in that large gymnasium, watching *him* walk across the stage to get *his* diploma. I was thinking, *He did it!* I was very proud of what he had accomplished. But I was proud of what I had accomplished, too."

It's been a long, hard road with many bitter but extremely valuable stops along the way. "When I think back on everything I've been through, from age 16 until today, I can say without hesitation that I would not have missed having my son for anything. Even more importantly, this whole experience led me to my Savior: He came to me when I was lonely and at my lowest point. I'm not sure how I would have met Him otherwise. But I always wonder, *What could I have been? Who would I have met? Could I have been a better mother? Could my kids have avoided some of the hardships they've had to face? Would I have waited for someone who really loved me, who had the capacity to be a good father to my children?*"

Leslie will never know the answers to her wistful questions. As the great lion Aslan told Lucy in C.S. Lewis's classic *The Chronicles of*

Narnia, "No one may know what *might* have happened." But what is Leslie's message to teens today? "I wish they could realize the incredible potential they have," she says. "And I wish they could understand that they're not ready for sex. It's not time yet.

"You need time to grow. You need to nurture yourself and bring yourself to the place where you can stand on your own. Only then will you really have something to share with the one person who is worthy to share your life. Save those coins in your pocket until they're worth something. Delay the decision to give yourself away to another person sexually for as long as you can. Delay it until marriage for the greatest benefits and highest returns.

"Abstinence," she adds, "is *powerful*. Abstinence is saying, 'I know who I am. I have plans. I have a future and I know where I'm going.'"

Adrienne: "There's a Reason I'm Still Here"

Adrienne's story doesn't build quite so dramatically. But then, Adrienne hasn't traveled as far as Leslie. At the time of this writing she's still sorting it all out. She has her good days and her bad; her life looks like a checkerboard of dark and light patches. But it also demonstrates that God can take a mixed and crazy pattern and make it into something beautiful.

Adrienne is finding out firsthand that having babies and raising kids is often a plain, unexciting, workaday kind of existence: a slow, steady, determined walk in a solitary direction. It's nothing like the free and independent college life she envisioned for herself as a carefree, fun-loving high school student. That's the down side. But the up side is that her life is filled with real-world lessons in integrity and responsibility and hard work. You can't put a price tag on that kind of experience.

Pain and regret? Oh yeah. Adrienne lives with more regrets than she could have imagined on that night of her sixteenth birthday. Regrets about her abortion. Regrets about the loss of her virginity. Regrets about missed opportunities and the life she let slip through her careless fingers.

Remember what Adrienne said in Chapter 4: "I wish every day of my life that I still had my virginity. I wish I had taken a stand to be abstinent and that the decision to have sex was a decision I still had to make. If I had to go back and do it all over again, I would definitely do things differently."

It can be hard for a young woman in that

position to *feel* that God loves her and forgives her. Emotions are volatile, sometimes even uncontrollable. But Adrienne realizes there's more to life and faith than just feelings. "I know in my head that I've been forgiven," she says, "and that God still has a really cool plan for me—that He saved my son and saved my life on purpose. It wasn't just an accident. There's a reason He gave that little boy to me. And there's a reason I'm still here. I take comfort in that."

So pain and regret are not the end of Adrienne's story. Far from it! And though it's not always easy for her, there are those moments when the light breaks through and she sees the bigger picture; moments when the veil is pulled aside and she is granted a vision of God's grace at work in her life. More often than not, she catches those glimpses of grace and wonder when she's looking at Justin—the son conceived as a result of her mistakes.

"Right after Justin was born I felt a closeness to God I hadn't felt in a very long time. I saw Justin as a gift from God, a miracle. I was so thankful that God had taken me through that experience, brought me to that place, and given me that child. For me, his birth was like a new beginning."

The birth of a baby. A fresh, new,

unstained life. A sign of hope and opportunity and possibility. A chance to start over, wipe the slate clean, and do it right this time—not only for her own sake, but also for the sake of the child entrusted to her care. All this and more is what God has given to Adrienne in exchange for the unwise management of her sexuality. No, it's not an even trade. But it *is* what grace is all about.

No matter how badly we mess up our lives, God can always bring good out of evil if we'll only trust Him. Looking at a child like Justin, it's easy to see that *God* doesn't make mistakes. With Him, *nothing* ever just "happens to happen."

Sarah: "I've Grown a Lot"

And what about Sarah? A mom at 19; separated from her baby's father by abuse, violence, shattered hopes, disillusionment, and immigration law; a high school dropout struggling to raise a child while attending cosmetology school; a Christian painfully conscious of having betrayed her own convictions. Does Sarah see any sense in the story of her life? Has she been able to pick out any bright and hopeful threads from the torn and shredded fabric of her fairy tale dream?

Like Adrienne, Sarah has days when she

feels as if she's walking in a fog. She too faces the challenge of slogging her way through the day-to-day problems and practicalities of her situation. Juggling work, school, mothering, and childcare. Sifting and sorting her own feelings about who she is, where she's come from, and where she's going. She's still dealing with the hurt, the disappointment, and the trauma of everything she's endured. And she's thinking about how she'll explain it all to Jimmy Jr. when *he's* 16 years old. That's important to her.

In fact, little Jimmy's presence in her life is like a focused lens through which she's able to review, reevaluate, and understand her own experience. As she ponders what she'll say to him about her journey, she sees its meaning all the more clearly for herself.

"I'll tell him that I thought I was immune. And I'll tell him that he is living proof that I was *not* immune, and that it's a hard world to live in. But if you're walking the right way and doing what you're supposed to do— well, it doesn't necessarily make it easier, but you won't have to deal with the negative consequences I've had to face."

Sarah's trying to walk in the right way herself. And she's beginning to see the silver lining behind the dark cloud that's hung over her head for the past few years. She knows that though she has been forced to deal with all sorts of problems and difficulties along the road she has traveled—obstacles of her own making—yet in some strange and wonderful way the overall pattern and plan belong to God. Most of all, she's aware that she is who she is today, at least in part, because of the hard and hurtful experiences she's endured. And that's a *good* thing.

"I've grown a lot. I believe I'm more mature. I do regret having sex before I married, but that's not to say that I regret having my baby. My baby's the greatest thing I could ever ask for."

Sarah's ordeal has led to another important side benefit—a benefit even she may have missed. Sarah, like Adrienne and Leslie, can become what author Henri Nouwen calls "a wounded healer." She's like an advance scout who goes ahead and checks out the territory, discovering, through personal tragedy, that sex before marriage is foolish. Now she's come back to warn the rest of the troops. She's been to the other side and brought back a dearly purchased message for the rest of us.

"Teens today," Sarah observes, "are just like me. They think they're immune. They might read my story and say, 'That's not going to happen to me.' But it can happen to them.

"Despite what you've heard, everybody is *not* doing it. Some people—especially guys—even lie about doing it to make themselves look cool. There's a warning for girls in that. Girls do it and they're sluts; guys do it and they're super studs. And it's not even worth getting the reputation. Everybody's *not* doing it. And you're not immune to what I've been through."

"A 26-year-old in a 19-year-old body"—that's how Sarah describes herself. She's made her share of mistakes. She has learned some crucial lessons the hard way. And at this point in her life, she's determined to put the past behind her and do what's right.

"I'm going to tell my future husband that I did make a mistake. I can't go back and change the hand of time, but I'm not going to lie about it. I'm going to be up-front and open. And from now on I will not have sex until I get married."

"No Apologies"—The Chance of a Lifetime

"We all stumble in many ways," writes the apostle James. Losing your virginity before marriage is just one of a million possibilities. It's serious. It's *sin*. It's a problem that needs to be addressed. But it's not the end of the line.

Here's the simple, exciting truth. You have been given a tremendous opportunity, an opportunity that renews itself constantly and never becomes obsolete. As long as you live on this earth it can never slip entirely beyond your grasp. It's an opportunity to put all the old slip-ups and sorrows and embarrassments behind you and move ahead with confidence into a hopeful future.

It's the chance of a lifetime. And you get it every day.

Here's the way it works. If you're still a virgin, then *stay* a virgin. At this very moment it lies within your power to keep yourself sexually pure, to save yourself for the man or woman who will one day share your life. You have the potential to present that special person with the greatest gift one human being can ever give another—yourself, complete, whole, and unspoiled. The choice is yours, and no power in earth or heaven is strong enough to deprive you of it.

If, on the other hand, you've been sexually active in the past, then decide now to make a change. It's *never* too late. Regaining control of yourself after engaging in premarital sex won't necessarily be easy, especially if you're still involved with the guy or girl who got you moving in that direction. But it *is* possible. A decision to remain abstinent may mean breaking off that relationship altogether. Whatever it takes, do it. It's crucial that you find a way to break the old patterns and establish new ones. If you want a new life badly enough, you can make it happen …with God's help.

And remember this: though you may have given up a very important part of yourself through premature sexual activity, God can restore it to you. He's the Lord of the whole universe, and He knows where those forfeited bits of your soul have gone—every last particle. He can gather the missing pieces, put them back in place, and make you whole again. If you ask Him, He *will* perform the miracle of soul surgery and fill you with a vision of what can happen when you belong to Him completely.

There's every reason in the world to make that commitment. Resisting the temptation to become sexually involved before marriage will enable you to do all of the following—and more:

- Achieve your goals and dreams.
- Be faithful and committed to your future spouse.
- Respect the health and well-being of other people's future spouses.
- Safeguard your reproductive health.

- Protect the health of your future children.
- Enjoy your teen years without the stress and pressure of a sexual relationship.

So take the pledge. Save yourself for marriage. Join Austin O'Brien and the thousands of other teens who have had the courage to make the following promise. And make it publicly:

Believing in *Saving Myself for Marriage,*
I make a commitment to myself,
my family, my friends,
my future spouse, and my
children to be sexually abstinent
from this day forward until
the day I enter a lifelong, committed,
monogamous marriage.

It's worth the effort. And you *can* do it.

We all mess up. We all go astray. We all do and say things we wish we'd never done or said. But God is bigger than our mistakes, and the treasure-store of His forgiveness in Jesus Christ is rich enough to cover *all* our debts. When we get to the last page of the book, there will be no apologies from *Him*—just a marvelously awe-inspiring and glorious explanation of the ways in which He's been guiding us, leading us, providing for us, and holding our lives in His hands from the very beginning. If we walk with Him, we'll eventually come to a place without blunders or errors—just an open door to a whole new heavenly world without tears, without regrets, and without apologies.

And that, friend, is incredibly good news.

Notes

Chapter 2

1. Floyd G. Brown, "Life and Death in Arkansas," *The National Review* (April 26, 1993): 38-39.

2. Suzanne Fields, "Listening to Elders and Saying No," *The Washington Times* (July 15, 1993): G1.

3. Gilbert L. Crouse, Office of Planning and Evaluation, U.S. Department of Health and Human Services, based on data from Planned Parenthood's Alan Guttmacher Institute (March 12, 1992): 23.

4. National Center for Health Statistics, Monthly Vital Statistics Report 41, no. 9 (February 25, 1993).

5. "Birthrate Soars at Colorado School," *USA Today* (May 19, 1992).

6. D. Fleming, et. al., "Herpes simplex virus type 2 in the United States, 1976-1994," *New England Journal of Medicine* 337, no. 16 (October 1997): 1105-11.

7. G.R. Burstein and C. A. Gaydos, et. al., "Chlamydia Trachomatis Infection Among Sexually Active Adolescent Females," *Journal of American Medical Association* 280: 521-26.

8. Kaiser Family Foundation, *Sexually Transmitted Diseases in America: How Many Cases and at What Cost?* (December 1998): 5.

9. Elizabeth Brown and William R. Hendee, "Adolescents and Their Music: Insights

into the Health of Adolescents," *The Journal of the American Medical Association* (September 22, 1989).

10. *Purr* magazine, no. 5, quoted by Bob Smithouser and Bob Waliszewski in *Chart Watch* (Wheaton, Ill.: Tyndale House Publishers, 1998): 16.

11. These quotations are cited by Bob Smithouser and Bob Waliszewski in *Chart Watch*: 9-10.

12. Ibid., 28.

13. Center of Addiction and Substance Abuse (CASA), New York's Columbia University Study, "Rethinking Rites of Passage: Substance Abuse on America's Campuses; A Report of the Commission on Substance Abuse at Colleges and Universities," (1994).

14. Robin Warshaw, *I Never Called It Rape* (New York: Harper Collins, 1988).

Chapter 3

1. The Alan Guttmacher Institute, *Sex and America's Teenagers* (New York, 1994): 20, 22-23.

2. Ibid.

3. F. L. Sonenstein, et. al., "Changes in sexual behavior and condom use among teenaged males: 1988 to 1995," *American Journal of Public Health* 88, no. 6 (June 1998): 956-59.

4. The Alan Guttmacher Institute, *Sex and America's Teenagers*: 19.
5. Ibid., 7.
6. Ibid., 27.
7. Centers for Disease Control and Prevention, "Youth risk behavior surveillance— United States, 1997," *Morbidity and Mortality Weekly Report* 47, no. SS-3 (1998).
8. The Alan Guttmacher Institute, *Sex and America's Teenagers*: 22-28.
9. James C. Dobson, *Life on the Edge* (Dallas, Tex.: Word Publishers, 1996): 93.
10. Stephen Arterburn, *Surprised by God* (Colorado Springs, Colo.: Focus on the Family Publishing, 1997): 55-56.
11. Dorothy V. Whipple, *Dynamics of Development: Euthenic Pediatrics* (New York: McGraw-Hill, 1966): 98.
12. Quoted on *Focus on the Family* daily radio broadcast, December 9, 1996. Focus on the Family, Colorado Springs, CO 80995.

Chapter 4

1. Grant Wahl and L. Jon Werthheim, "Paternity Ward," *Sports Illustrated* 88, no. 18 (May 4, 1998): 69.

Chapter 5

1. Tina Huffman on Focus on the Family daily radio broadcast, "A Matter of Life," January 18, 1995. Focus on the Family, Colorado Springs, CO 80995.

2. Joe White, *Pure Excitement* (Colorado Springs, Colo.: Focus on the Family Publishing, 1996): 75.

3. Kaiser Family Foundation, *Sexually Transmitted Diseases in America: How Many Cases and at What Cost?* (December 1998): 5.

4. Centers for Disease Control and Prevention, "Sexually transmitted disease surveillance 1995," *Morbidity and Mortality Weekly Report* 45, no. 53 (September 1996).

5. U. S. Department of Health and Human Services, Division of HIV/STD Prevention Annual Report (1991): 5.

6. A. E. Washington and P. Katz, "Cost of and Payment Source for Pelvic Inflammatory Disease," *Journal of the American Medical Association* 266, no. 18: 2565-69.

7. Centers for Disease Control (CDC), "Centers for Disease Control Division of STD/HIV 1991 Annual Report," (1992): 3.

8. Kaiser Family Foundation, *Sexually Transmitted Diseases in America: How Many Cases and at What Cost?* (December 1998): 5-6.

9. Gloria Ho, et. al., "Natural History of Cervicovaginal Papillomavirus Infection in Young Women," *The New England Journal of Medicine* 338, no. 7 (1998): 423-28.

10. Letter to Focus on the Family, quoted on the Focus on the Family daily radio broadcast "A Doctor Speaks Out on Sexually Transmitted Diseases," June 5, 1996. Focus on the Family, Colorado Springs, CO 80995.

11. E. F. Jones and J. D. Forrest, "Contraceptive Failure Rates Based on the 1988 NSFG," *Family Planning Perspectives* 24, no. 1 (1998): 12-19.

12. R. Hatcher, et. al., *Contraceptive Technology*, 17th ed. (Irvington Publishers).

13. E.F. Jones and J.D. Forrest, "Contraceptive Failure Rates Based on the 1988 NSFG," *Family Planning Perspectives* (January/February 1992): 12-19.

14. Centers for Disease Control and Prevention, "Condoms for Prevention of Sexually Transmitted Disease," *Morbidity and Mortality Weekly Report* 37, no. 9 (March 11, 1998): 133-37.

15. "Vulvar Diseases: An Expert Panel Answers Questions," *The Colposcopist* 26, no. 3 (Summer 1995): 3.

16. I. deVincenzi, "A Longitudinal Study of Immunodeficiency Virus Transmission by Heterosexual Partners," *The New England Journal of Medicine* 331, no. 6 (1994): 341-46.

17. A. Saracco et. al., "Man-to-Woman Sexual Transmission of HIV: Longitudinal Study of 343 Steady Partners of Infected Men," *Journal of Acquired Immune Deficiency Syndromes* 6, no. 5 (1993): 497-502.

18. Centers for Disease Control, "Update: Barrier Protections Against HIV Infection and Other Sexually Transmitted Diseases," *Morbidity and Mortality Weekly Report* 42, no. 30 (August 6, 1993): 589-97.

19. William G. Axinn and Arland Thornton, "Mothers, Children, and Cohabitation: The Intergenerational Effects of Attitudes and Behaviors," *American Sociological Review* 58 (September 1993): 233-46.

Chapter 6

1. Center for Population Options, "The Facts: School-Based Clinics," (June 1990).
2. Dinah Richard, *Has Sex Education Failed Our Teenagers? A Research Report* (Pomona, Calif.: Focus on the Family Publishing, 1990): 4.
3. Heather Jamison, "She's Not Wearing White," *Youthworker* (May/June 1998): 51-52.

Chapter 8

1. Joe White, *Pure Excitement* (Colorado Springs, Colo.: Focus on the Family Publishing, 1996): 12-13.
2. Kristi Collier Thompson, "I Need Another Fig Leaf: Fighting Sexual Temptation," *Brio* (July 1997): 34.
3. Joshua Harris, *I Kissed Dating Goodbye* (Sisters, Ore.: Multnomah Publishers, 1997): 95-96.
4. James C. Dobson, *Solid Answers* (Wheaton, Ill.: Tyndale House Publishers, 1997), Question #343.
5. Jim Talley and Bobbie Reed, *Too Close, Too Soon* (Nashville, Tenn.: Thomas Nelson Publishers, 1982).

6. White, *Pure Excitement*, 36-37.
7. Bob Smithouser and Bob Waliszewski, *Chart Watch* (Wheaton, Ill.: Tyndale House Publishers, 1998): 19-20.
8. James C. Dobson, *Love for a Lifetime* (Sisters, Ore.: Multnomah Publishers, 1987): 20.
9. Harris, *I Kissed Dating Goodbye*, 31.
10. Randy Alcorn, "Sexual Purity: What You Need to Do." *Eternal Perspective Ministries Quarterly Newsletter* (spring 1998).
11. Harris, *I Kissed Dating Goodbye*: 46-50.

Chapter 9
1. National Longitudinal Study on Adolescent Health, "Protecting Adolescents from Harm," *The Journal of the American Medical Association* (September 1997): 830.

FOCUS ON THE FAMILY®
Welcome to the Family!

Whether you received this book as a gift, borrowed it from
a friend, or purchased it yourself, we're glad you read it!
It's just one of the many helpful, insightful, and encouraging
resources produced by Focus on the Family.

In fact, that's what Focus on the Family is all about—
providing inspiration, information, and biblically based
advice to people in all stages of life.

It began in 1977 with the vision of one man, Dr. James Dobson,
a licensed psychologist and author of 16 best-selling books on
marriage, parenting, and family. Alarmed by the societal, political,
and economic pressures that were threatening the existence
of the American family, Dr. Dobson founded Focus on the Family
with one employee—an assistant—and a once-a-week
radio broadcast, aired on only 36 stations.

Now an international organization, Focus on the Family is
dedicated to preserving Judeo-Christian values and strengthening
the family through more than 70 different ministries, including
eight separate daily radio broadcasts; television public service
announcements; 11 publications; and a steady series of
award-winning books, films, and videos for people
of all ages and interests.

Recognizing the needs of, as well as the sacrifices and important
contribution made by, such diverse groups as educators, physicians, attorneys, crisis pregnancy center staff, and single parents,
Focus on the Family offers specific outreaches to uphold and minister to these individuals, too. And it's all done for one purpose,
and one purpose only: to encourage and strengthen individuals
and families through the life-changing message of Jesus Christ.

• • •

For more information about the ministry, or if we can be of help to
your family, simply write to Focus on the Family, Colorado Springs,
CO 80995 or call 1-800-A-FAMILY (1-800-232-6459). Friends in
Canada may write Focus on the Family, P.O. Box 9800, Stn. Termi-
nal, Vancouver, B.C. V6B 4G3 or call 1-800-661-9800. Visit our Web
site—www.family.org—to learn more about the ministry or to find
out if there is a Focus on the Family office in your country.

We'd love to hear from you!